What Your Colleagues Are S

"As we strive for high levels of learning—and colleg
for all students, co-teaching has never been as important. No one
has as much to offer in guiding educators to success within inclusive,
differentiated environments than Angela Peery. This book will be your
trusted resource."

Chris Weber, EdD
Irvine Unified School District
Irvine, CA

"Practitioners can use this workbook as a tool to get a good start on team
teaching/co-teaching. It is well organized and well thought out. The
personal experiences and vignettes are all relevant and show the good,
the bad, and the ugly. It will be a big help to beginners and for those
who want a second chance at making it work."

Claudia A. Danna
Curriculum Director
Sacred Heart University

"This book is an excellent resource for teachers new to co-teaching. It is
a resource both teachers should use to learn about each other and their
teaching styles so they can ensure their classroom environment and
teaching best serves their students."

Stacy Lemongelli
District Instructional Leader, ELA
Perth Amboy Public Schools District

"*The Co-Teacher's Playbook* is one of those rare occasions where the
content delivers on the promise of the title. I don't know of a single
other book on this topic that ties it together so well and in such a
clear fashion though the use of tools, activities, and the clear, easy
connections Dr. Peery has made. She has crafted a text that is applicable
for those new to co-teaching with clear definitions and activities at each
step, while also challenging veterans of the practice by sharing practical
insights and extension activities. With this book Dr. Peery has moved
the important work of co-teaching from novelty (practiced by a few,
passionate educators) to necessity."

Tom Hierck
Educator and Speaker
Author, *Grading for Impact*

"The Co-Teacher's Playbook is essential reading for making co-teaching a reality. Dr. Peery offers a comprehensive framework for successful implementation. Her book is a must read for any team contemplating a co-teaching model."

Ajit "AJ" Pethe
Assistant Superintendent
Curriculum, Instruction and Assessment
St. Charles Parish Public Schools

The Co-Teacher's Playbook

The Co-Teacher's Playbook

What It Takes to Make Co-Teaching Work for Everyone

Angela Peery

FOR INFORMATION:

Corwin
A SAGE Company
2455 Teller Road
Thousand Oaks, California 91320
(800) 233-9936
www.corwin.com

SAGE Publications Ltd.
1 Oliver's Yard
55 City Road
London EC1Y 1SP
United Kingdom

SAGE Publications India Pvt. Ltd.
B 1/I 1 Mohan Cooperative Industrial Area
Mathura Road, New Delhi 110 044
India

SAGE Publications Asia-Pacific Pte. Ltd.
18 Cross Street #10-10/11/12
China Square Central
Singapore 048423

Acquisitions Editor: Ariel Curry
Development Editor: Desirée A. Bartlett
Associate Content Development
      Editor: Jessica Vidal
Production Editor: Jane Martinez
Copy Editor: Shannon Kelly
Typesetter: C&M Digitals (P) Ltd.
Proofreader: Annie Lubinsky
Indexer: Terri Morrissey
Cover and Graphic Designer: Anupama Krishnan
Marketing Manager: Margaret O'Connor

Printed in the United States of America.

Library of Congress Cataloging-in-Publication Data

Names: Peery, Angela B., author.

Title: The co-teacher's playbook : what it takes to make co-teaching work for everyone / Angela Peery, Whale Branch Middle School.

Description: Thousand Oaks, California : Corwin, ICLE [2020] | Includes bibliographical references and index.

Identifiers: LCCN 2019011377 | ISBN 9781544377629 (spiral)

Subjects: LCSH: Teaching teams—United States. | Team learning approach in education—United States. | Special education—Study and teaching—United States.

Classification: LCC LB1029.T4 P44 2020 | DDC 371.14/8—dc23
LC record available at https://lccn.loc.gov/2019011377

This book is printed on acid-free paper.

SUSTAINABLE FORESTRY INITIATIVE

Certified Chain of Custody
Promoting Sustainable Forestry
www.sfiprogram.org
SFI-01268

SFI label applies to text stock

19 20 21 22 23 10 9 8 7 6 5 4 3 2 1

Contents

Visit the companion website at
http://resources.corwin.com/coteachersplaybook
for downloadable resources.

Acknowledgments

A book never materializes from the writer alone; there are scores of collaborators all along the way and folks from the past who, at the time, never knew they were such an important part of the story.

I offer my deepest gratitude to Harriet Blanton, Joan Grimmett, and Sandie Merriam, my colleagues at North Myrtle Beach High School in South Carolina, who first engaged in co-teaching efforts with me. Harriet was our principal and had the vision to pair special education teachers with me (an English teacher) in order to better serve our ninth-grade students. Joan and Sandie were my co-teaching partners. What we were doing over twenty years ago is finally catching on in popularity! It's about time!

Educators Ashley Blackley, Melissa Eddington, Justin Garcia, Anabel Gonzalez, Rebecca Matherne, and Jennifer Wolf contributed greatly to this book. Teachers at Washington High School in Massillon, OH; at R. K. Smith Middle School in St. Charles Parish, LA; and at Episcopal Academy in Newtown Square, PA, have all shaped this text as well. I have grown immensely from my collaboration with all these caring, reflective educators.

I also appreciate conversations I've had with Jennifer Gonzalez and Andrea Honigsfeld about co-teaching. These two author/educators are important voices in the field. Follow them on social media and read everything they have written—trust me, they are that good.

Lastly, even though my husband has stopped reading the acknowledgments that I mention him in, I will once again thank him for the dozens of ways he both tolerated and supported me during the writing of this book. My thirty-three years of being an educator coincide with thirty-three years of being with him, and I know that in that long period of time he has sometimes felt that he comes in second to the work. Tim, you've made me a better teacher and a better person, and you're first. Always.

Publisher's Acknowledgments

Corwin gratefully acknowledges the contributions of the following reviewers:

Helene Alalouf
Education Consultant
NYC Schools
New York, NY

Erin Baker
Literacy Trainer PreK–6th
Missouri Reading Initiative
Springfield, MO

Claudia A. Danna
Curriculum Director
Sacred Heart University
Griswold, CT

Sarah Gat
Instructional Coach
Upper Grand District School Board
Ontario, Canada

Stacy Lemongelli
District Instructional Leader, ELA
Perth Amboy Public Schools District
Amboy, NJ

John F. Mahoney
2005 Inductee: National Teachers Hall of Fame
Lecturer in Mathematics
Montgomery College
Rockville, MD

Elvira Pichardo-Delacour
Instructional Specialist (K–5)
Mathematics and Bilingual Education
Berwyn North School District 98
Berwyn, IL

Jennifer Reichel
Director of Teaching and Learning
Hastings Public Schools
Hastings, MN

About the Author

Dr. Angela Peery is a consultant and author with over thirty years of experience as an educator. She has spent the last decade completing over 100 speaking and consulting days per year and authoring or co-authoring fourteen books, including the bestsellers *Writing Matters in Every Classroom* and *The Data Teams Experience: A Guide for Effective Meetings*.

Prior to becoming a consultant, Angela was an instructional coach for a chronically low-performing middle school. Her other experience includes ten years of classroom teaching in middle and high schools, four years as a high school administrator, and leadership roles at the building, district, and state levels. In these roles, she developed curricula and mentored other teachers in standards implementation. She also taught undergraduate and graduate courses, both in person and online. Additionally, she was co-director of a National Writing Project site for several years, teaching the summer institute.

Angela earned her doctorate in curriculum in 2000. Her doctoral research highlighted professional development in literacy that she facilitated with teachers at a K–8 Jewish day school.

A Virginia native, Angela earned her B. A. in English at Randolph-Macon Woman's College and her M. A. in liberal arts at Hollins College. Her professional licensures include secondary English, secondary administration, and gifted/talented education. She has also studied presentation design and delivery with experts Nancy Duarte, Garr Reynolds, and Rick Altman. Recently, she has undertaken graduate study in brain-based learning and global education.

Angela makes her home in Beaufort, South Carolina, with her husband of thirty years, Tim, and their pets. When not traveling and working with educators, she most enjoys being on her boat or attending rock concerts. She can be reached at drangelapeery@gmail.com.

INTRODUCTION
WHY THIS BOOK, AND WHY ME?

Welcome to *The Co-Teacher's Playbook: What It Takes to Make Co-Teaching Work for Everyone*. I'd like to introduce you to this book and to me in this short introduction.

I've been an educator since 1986, and I've served in a huge variety of roles. For the last fifteen years, I've been a full-time author and consultant, and in that capacity, I've supported hundreds of teachers, many of whom are in co-teaching relationships. In the seventeen years prior to my consulting career, I was a teacher, administrator, and instructional coach. During two of my years as a high school English teacher, I was part of a co-teaching team, paired with a special education teacher each time.

My co-teaching experience had ups and downs. Both of my special education partners were a joy to collaborate with, but we struggled with the same issues I see many teams struggling with today—communication between us, communication with parents, equitable grading, a lack of planning time, and the list goes on.

Based on my own co-teaching journey and how it has intersected with and informed my consulting, I offer this book to you so that you can become more effective at any point in a co-teaching situation. This book is intended to be most useful if read together by a co-teaching pair so that both teachers can discuss the information, complete the activities, and use the tools. You'll find that the text is meant to be conversational and direct in speaking to you, and you'll see that the various activities and tools are meant to be used as you best see fit. The overarching goal is for you and your co-teaching partner to use this book as a vital support in your ongoing professional growth.

You may have had time to plan and prepare for a new school year ahead of time as a co-teaching pair, or you may have just had the arrangement sprung upon you with seemingly no lead time. Either situation is fine. I'll strive to present the ideal scenarios within this book, but I'll also make every effort to address the not-so-ideal situations that I see many of my teaching colleagues in.

The book consists of four distinct types of material:

1. Text

2. Activities

3. Tools

4. Extensions

Text often appears first in each chapter and consists of necessary information and explanation. So, text might include definitions, characteristics, summary, and even vignettes of effective or ineffective co-teaching. Text tees up what follows (activities, tools, and extensions) and often also provides some instruction to be applied in the activities and via the tools.

Most activities are designed to be completed individually either during or after the reading of the text, as indicated by their placement. Ideally, co-teaching partners will discuss their responses. Some activities are designed to be completed with your co-teaching partner or to be used in a group setting. All the activities are intended to get you processing the content of the text at a deeper level and personalizing it to your unique situation.

Tools are lists, checklists, letters, templates, agreements, and other documents to be directly applied to the day-to-day workings of co-teaching. You can use the documents exactly as they appear or choose to modify them to best fit your unique situation. Both reproducible "as is" and changeable versions of the forms appear online at http://resources.corwin.com/coteachersplaybook.

Extensions are recommended readings and activities that take you beyond the text and deeper into content you may be interested in. Each extension includes at least a brief annotation or summary and recommendations for how it could be used by you and your co-teaching partner.

This book is designed to be worked through from beginning to end with your co-teaching partner. If you are part of more than one co-teaching partnership, you may find that it's easiest (and most valuable) to explore the text and work through the exercises with only one co-teaching partner at a time. If you choose to read the book with more than one co-teaching partner, or if you're part of a book study or a class using the book, you'll find that the text portions and recommended readings may be most meaningful for group discussion.

Co-teaching can be one of the most powerful professional learning experiences of your career. However, for many co-teaching pairs, there can be confusion and frustration at times. This book will provide you with information and interactive tools that are intended to reduce confusion and frustration and to buoy you toward your highest level of effectiveness.

UNDERSTANDING

Introduction

Welcome to co-teaching! We'll start in this first chapter with information about what co-teaching is and how it looks in classrooms today. You'll also find exercises to get you started or, if you're an experienced co-teacher, to help you refine your understanding. Let's begin.

What Is Co-Teaching?

You've found yourself as part of a co-teaching pair, or perhaps you've found yourself as a partner to several other teachers (so, you're a member of several pairs). Regardless of how you came to be involved in such a collaborative relationship, this book is intended to help deepen both your knowledge and expertise. Let's start by defining what co-teaching is. We'll also differentiate it from other teacher collaborations you may have experienced or that may be present in your school.

The definition of co-teaching that will be used in this book is as follows: Co-teaching is a teaching arrangement in which a generalist and a specialist employ their expertise jointly to maximize learning for all students, including those with identified disabilities, language deficits, and other special needs.

With this definition in mind, certain characteristics of effective co-teaching are implied. First, because the teachers must jointly instruct, some amount of common planning time is necessary. (This issue will be explored in greater detail in the coming pages.) Second, both teachers must have a solid grasp of differentiation. "One-size-fits-all" curriculum, instruction, and assessment simply are not compatible with the idea of effective co-teaching.

One of my professional mentors in co-teaching is Marilyn Friend. The following fundamental attributes of co-teaching originate in her work (2007):

- Co-teaching is a service delivery mechanism that includes two or more professionals with equivalent licensure and employment status participating.

- Co-teaching is based on parity; therefore, a parent volunteer, paraprofessional, or other adult who does not enjoy a similar status or salary is generally not considered a co-teacher but is instead considered support personnel.

- Co-teachers share the responsibility for the group(s) of students they serve. So, if I were currently a member of a co-teaching team, the students are not "my" kids or "your" kids, but are "our" kids. This means that both teachers must deal not only with instruction but also with classroom management, grading, and other concerns.

- Co-teaching occurs primarily in a shared classroom or workspace. Students are generally not pulled out to receive instruction in another physical location. This is a critical aspect of honoring the least restrictive environment requirement for students with identified disabilities.

Read the other common definitions of co-teaching below.

- "Co-teaching is the practice of pairing teachers together in a classroom to share the responsibilities of planning, instructing, and assessing students. In a co-teaching setting, the teachers are considered equally responsible and accountable for the classroom" (Trites, 2017).

- "The general definition of co-teaching involves two equally qualified individuals who may or may not have the same area of expertise jointly delivering instruction to a group of students. . . . For an instructional arrangement to be considered a co-teaching format, both partners must participate fully in the instruction" (Curry School of Education, 2012).

- "Co-teaching is utilizing two or more professionals with equivalent licensure that share instructional responsibility and accountability for a single group of students for whom they both have ownership" (Wisconsin Department of Public Instruction, n.d.).

Activity: What's Your Definition?

Complete the Frayer model graphic organizer below independently. Ideally, meet with your co-teaching partner to compare graphic organizers and to generate additional ideas. Once you've completed the Frayer model, try to come up with a shared definition that you both can refer to.

Your own definition of co-teaching	Critical attributes or characteristics
(Consider all the definitions in addition to what you'd add.)	*(What must be evident? What must be in place?)*
Examples of co-teaching	**Nonexamples of co-teaching**
(Think about what you've seen or experienced in your teaching career.)	*(Think about things that may look like co-teaching but that are not.)*

Source: Adapted from Frayer, Frederick, and Klausmeier (1969).

Our Shared Definition

Benefits of Co-Teaching

Why do schools and systems move to a model of co-teaching? Why upset the apple cart and pair teachers together instead of simply assigning one teacher per classroom as it's always been done? There are benefits that teachers often mention and feel are huge positives, although large-scale research into these benefits remains mixed.

Both academic gains and social/behavioral improvements are often reported anecdotally by teachers, but the hard data has been mixed (as summarized in Van Garderen, Stormont, & Goel, 2012). In a meta-analysis by Murawski and Swanson (2001), the overall mean effect size was 0.40, a statistically significant finding that suggests co-teaching is moderately effective. However, the caution here is the word *moderately*. Because there are so many variables with co-teaching, and because so few large-scale studies have been completed on the practice, sweeping generalizations simply can't be made.

Speaking from my experience as a co-teacher whose classes were filled with overage boys who had individualized education programs (IEPs) in reading, I agree with teachers who see both academic and social gains in co-taught classes. Many of the male students I taught had been written off by other teachers as virtually unteachable, yet my co-teacher and I were able to support them in raising not only their reading levels but also their academic confidence in general. Many of my students started earning good grades not only in our class but in their other classes as well.

Often teachers cite as a benefit the fact that special education students and English language learners get to see, hear, and participate in higher-level academic conversation when in co-taught classes rather than when in pull-out situations. Melissa Eddington, an ELL teacher who has been in co-teaching situations, says that she appreciates her students having peer models of academic vocabulary and standard grammar and syntax when in co-taught classes. Eddington also notes that her students feel like "one of the rest" in co-taught classes, meaning that they do not feel separated or different. This is a phenomenon I too have experienced; students who would have normally been pulled out for support or who would have had an entirely separate and below-grade-level English class sat right beside their on-grade-level peers in my classroom, and I expected them to fully take part in reading, speaking, writing, and collaboration activities. In most cases, they stepped up to the plate with energy and enthusiasm.

Students without specific disabilities often get to experience differentiation and collaboration differently when in co-taught classes. Anabel Gonzalez, an ELL specialist who has worked as part of two co-teaching teams, notes that regular ed students often benefit from literacy strategies employed in co-teaching that may not have been used by the regular ed teacher alone. I agree; innovation benefitting all students is often a realized benefit. Co-teaching pairs often report to me that sharing innovative ideas between them is one of the best features of the relationship.

Deeper understanding and increased empathy are benefits that are also often cited in the research. As a co-teacher myself, I witnessed my general ed students being incredibly kind, patient, and collaborative with my special needs students, even those who had conditions (like Tourette's syndrome) that made it difficult for whole-class or group work to flow smoothly at times. I also saw my special needs students grow in assurance and participate equally and brilliantly in academic tasks with their non–special needs peers.

Some research studies report positive results and mirror my own experiences. For example, students with disabilities served in inclusive settings showed improvement on standardized tests as well as increased social and communication skills (Power-DeFur & Orelove, 1997). They enjoyed more frequent and higher-quality interaction with peers and, by some measures, were better prepared for postschool academic and work experiences (Power-DeFur & Orelove, 1997; Sharpe, n.d.).

Van Garderen and colleagues (2012) summed up the findings well when they said that there is a trend toward positive outcomes from inclusion or push-in models, but even when outcomes seem mixed, we should not interpret this to mean that a model is "bad." They suggest that lesser outcomes simply mean that more typical practices in some situations, like pull-out services, may be just as effective in supporting students.

Justin Garcia (2018b), an ELL co-teacher, presents a compelling argument for how co-teaching can benefit both teachers and students:

> I've only been co-teaching for a few months, [but] I'm already seeing the huge benefits of this model on language learners and teachers. Teachers have become more collaborative in their day-to-day practice, and students have benefited from having content and language instruction interwoven throughout lesson activities. . . . Another colleague pointed out how having me be present in her classroom has helped her learn unique ELL strategies that she has never thought of before. Too often

are we left in our classrooms to our own devices with our doors shut. As we know, teaching is a highly collaborative profession; new methods and research are constantly developing every year, and it can be difficult to keep up to date with all of the modern jargon. Collaborating with colleagues eases this load as research and methods are shared and practiced together instead of individually.

Ashley Blackley, a first-grade co-teacher, offered a personal observation via e-mail about how co-teaching benefits students: "The best part about co-teaching is that the students have no idea why they are in the class. They aren't being pulled out and embarrassed that they receive support. And they also never miss important content that they need to be there for."

The key idea from the mixed research is that co-teaching is one of several options that may work well in serving special needs students. School leaders must determine when, why, and how co-teaching might work and for whom it might be best.

Activity: The Benefits of Co-Teaching

Reflect on what you just read. Envision your class(es) and think about what you see. Record your ideas below.

Benefits I would like for my special needs/ELL students to realize:	Benefits I would like for my regular ed students to realize:

Additionally, you may want to think about how you will benefit from having another teacher in the room with you. For example, do you look forward to learning new instructional strategies? Jot a few ideas below about how co-teaching will benefit you as a professional.

Co-Teaching: What Does It Look Like in Today's Classrooms?

Educators know that classrooms of today look different from the past in many respects—the technology used, the seating and other furniture in the room, even the clothing the students wear and the slang they use in speaking with each other. However, many things appear unchanged from a century or more ago, most notably the fact that often one adult stands at the front of the room, speaking to a large group of students who nod, listen (or pretend to listen), and write things down periodically, sometimes after a reminder from the adult to do so.

Co-teaching classrooms look remarkably different from the traditional classroom in which one teacher works mostly independently. In today's classrooms, there are quite a few different co-teaching partnerships, even though the most common and well-researched one is the one between a generalist and a special education specialist. The most common forms of partnerships are described briefly below.

General Ed and Special Ed Partnerships

The longest-standing and most well-researched type of partnership is the one in which a general education teacher and a special education teacher are paired together. This partnership may look different based on the grade levels and licensures of each teacher, but at its core, it is simply this: One teacher is trained and/or has experience in teaching large groups of students, and the other is trained and/or has experience in focusing on individuals and their unique needs according to a specialized educational plan (such as an IEP or 504 plan in the United States).

The intent of this kind of partnership is to make it possible for students with identified disabilities to fully access the general curriculum while also benefiting from specialized instruction that is legally required and that is also recognized as effective instruction. In other words, this type of partnership makes it clear that both disabled and nondisabled students deserve the best instruction they can get, period, and that by having two teachers collaborate, both populations will be well served in the classroom. In this partnership, both teachers are responsible for instruction and assessment. The generalist may be the one who assumes the content leadership role and/or plans most of the curriculum, while the special education teacher's usual role is to be a strategy expert. He or she can often provide an abundance of ideas about adapting the lesson for a wide range of learners and can serve as an expert on how to reach individuals when it seems no strategy used thus far has worked.

General Ed and ESL/ELL Partnerships

Perhaps the next most common co-teaching arrangement is that of a generalist and a specialist in English language learning. The intent of this type of partnership is similar to that of the generalist and special education specialist: It is fundamental to both types of setups that no student be excluded from the regular curriculum because of a disability or (perceived) deficiency. The lack of full fluency in oral or written English should not hinder any student from participating fully in the general curriculum. In this partnership, as in the one described above, the generalist may be mostly responsible for curriculum matters like creating the learning goals, pacing the content, and ensuring full coverage of standards, while the English learning specialist might best contribute how to teach domain-specific vocabulary, how to provide language scaffolds and other supports, and how to incorporate plenty of oral language practice in lessons.

General Ed and Interventionist Partnerships

Partnerships between generalists and interventionists (for example, reading specialists) are still rare, but with staffing and funding changes in the last decade, these arrangements seem to be more common. The combination of the generalist and specialist allows each to contribute his or her expertise, as in the previously mentioned partnerships. The specialist may find that working with larger groups of students is quite a change because many are accustomed to small tutoring groups or working one-on-one with students. However, specialists are often able to share specific small-group strategies or highly specialized strategies for specific disabilities. This kind of expertise is often a wonderful complement to the "mass audience" kind of instruction that general education teachers are well schooled in and sometimes rely on too much.

General Ed and Specialist Partnerships

Growing in frequency is the co-teaching relationship that pairs a specialist like a technology integration or arts integration person with a general ed teacher. The specialist has specific, unique expertise that can well complement the expertise of the other teacher. In these relationships, the specialist may be partnered with more than one general ed teacher. For example, a technology specialist might work with one or two entire grade levels. This type of arrangement requires extremely careful planning.

General Ed and Paraprofessional Partnerships

As cited earlier (Friend, 2007), *co-teaching* is a term technically applied to two professionals who are equally licensed, and thus paraprofessionals are not considered co-teachers. They are considered support personnel. However, as staffing and funding challenges force administrators to become increasingly creative in how they structure teaching, these types of partnerships are cropping up more frequently. This type of relationship, by law and by licensure, is not a relationship of parity; the licensed teacher has responsibility for instruction and assessment. Parallel teaching and team teaching are generally not options for this pair because the credentialed teacher is the clear content expert.

Activity: Taking Stock

Complete the following together as a co-teaching team.

Teacher #1

I am a(n) _ _ _ _ _ _ _ _ _ _ _ _ _ _ _
teacher. (What do you most frequently
call yourself? For example, I would say,
"I am an English teacher.")

Teacher #2

I am a(n) _ _ _ _ _ _ _ _ _ _ _ _ _ _
teacher. (What do you most frequently
call yourself? My former co-teacher
Sandie would have said, "I'm a special ed
teacher who works with students who
are identified LD.")

Teacher #1

The best thing I bring to this partnership
is _.

Teacher #2

The best thing I bring to this partnership
is _.

Teacher #1

What are three things you're looking
forward to this year?

1.

2.

3.

Teacher #2

What are three things you're looking
forward to this year?

1.

2.

3.

Co-Teaching Structures

The most common names for the ways that two teachers partner together originate
in the work of Lynne Cook and Marilyn Friend in 1995 and have appeared in
many subsequent sources. The names of the six structures as first proposed by
Cook and Friend are as follows:

1. One teach, one assist

2. One teach, one observe

3. Alternative teaching

4. Parallel teaching

5. Station teaching

6. Team teaching

Consider the descriptions of each of the structures below and discuss with your co-teaching partner. (These descriptions are based on the original criteria from Friend and Cook and on my personal experience in working with co-teaching teams.)

1. ONE TEACH, ONE ASSIST

This particular structure is quite common among co-teachers and is definitely the number one favorite I see among pairs in secondary schools. It consists of one teacher leading instruction for the whole group while the other teacher circulates and helps students better understand and actively engage. The teacher assisting may provide hints, cues, and additional, more probing questions. He or she may also restate or rephrase what the lead teacher says so that students better understand. The assisting role should not be used primarily for behavior monitoring, although the assisting teacher can (and should) redirect students who are off task or disengaged. The assisting role should also not be one that I call a "glorified aide." In other words, the assisting teacher should not be stapling papers, creating bulletin boards, or other such menial tasks. At all times, the assisting teacher should be working to advance student understanding.

2. ONE TEACH, ONE OBSERVE

This structure may initially appear to be similar to *one teach, one assist*, but at its core, it is substantially different. Students remain in one large group while one teacher leads instruction and the other observes the lead teacher, the whole class, individual students, and/or small groups of students. The main objective for the observing teacher is to collect data that will ultimately improve instruction. Therefore, some options for observation include tallying the number of questions posed, recording how many different students are answering, noting who is disengaged and why, analyzing how groups work together, and studying how a struggling student responds during class. As in *one teach, one assist*, the observing teacher must be engaged in productive, data-gathering actions and not menial tasks, or valuable time will be wasted. The use of this structure also necessitates that the teachers meet together as soon as possible after class to discuss and act upon the data that was collected.

3. ALTERNATIVE TEACHING

This structure divides students into two groups, with one group usually being substantially smaller. The large group is led by one teacher as the other teacher works with the small group. The small group receives teaching that is unlike that of the large group (hence the word *alternative*). The small group members may receive instruction designed to prepare them for upcoming content or to reteach prior content that they did not master. The small group formation is ideally based on recent formative assessment data, whether that data is from a formal assessment or from informal assessment like teacher observation. Two reminders about alternative teaching: one, the formation of groups is flexible and in no way should relegate special needs students to a small group repeatedly; and two, both groups remain in close proximity to each other, preferably still within the same room, so that there is not a stigma associated with being in the small group. In teaching pairs that use alternative teaching often, care should be taken so that one teacher is not always with the small group and the other with the large group. The two professionals should continually demonstrate to students that they work in equal roles.

4. PARALLEL TEACHING

This formation again divides the entire class into two groups, but unlike alternative teaching, in parallel teaching the class is divided basically in half, and very similar (if not exact) content is being taught to each group. The specific methods or materials may differ. For example, Teacher A and Teacher B are teaching an introductory lesson on the replication of DNA. Teacher A uses lecture along with a partially filled-in Cornell notes template, PowerPoint slides, and short video clips with animation to show the process of replication. Teacher B, however, gives each student several pipe cleaners and beads to use as she describes and demonstrates replication. She supplements instruction with some large visuals displayed on the interactive whiteboard.

5. STATION TEACHING

Station teaching involves different areas to which students and teachers move, but it is not like centers, which are often seen in the primary grades. According to Marilyn Friend (Rosenthal & Zindler, 2015), each teacher takes his or her group(s) to various stations at different times; the teachers do not rotate from station to station. In practice, however, many teachers have modified this model and sometimes do indeed stay stationary as groups of heterogeneously mixed students rotate among stations. A common configuration is to have one or two stations where students work independently or with a paraprofessional while the other two stations are staffed by the co-teachers.

6. TEAM TEACHING

Team teaching is what many teachers with whom I work consider the ideal, but it is not always necessary or appropriate. However, when done well, it is incredibly effective. Team teaching is when both individuals teach collaboratively, playing off each other and jumping in on the lesson in what seems like a well-orchestrated waltz. Thus, pre-planning and even actual rehearsal are necessary to make this particular structure work. The co-teachers must be equally confident and competent in the content being presented, in the methods being used, and in the materials and technology being utilized during the lesson.

Reflection Questions

1. Which of the structures seem most comfortable for you?

2. Which structures do you expect that the two of you will use most often? Why?

3. What connections do you see between certain structures and content that you know you'll be teaching?

Conclusion

This chapter lays the groundwork for your work as a co-teacher. You are now familiar with the formal definitions of co-teaching, the various ways two professionals can be paired in co-teaching, and the six basic structures that co-teachers most often use. If you're interested in the history of co-teaching, you'll find a discussion of that in Appendix A. Appendix B contains handy visuals of the six co-teaching structures; you may want to use it as a reference during unit and lesson planning. See the tools and extensions that follow for more helpful information. Best wishes to you on this fantastic journey!

Tool 1   Welcome Letter to Students Template

Dear Student,

Welcome to a new school year! We are thrilled to have you as our student!

You may not have had a class shared by two teachers before. This is called co-teaching. Most of the time, we will be in the room together. You can come to either one of us at any time for help.

We would like to tell you a little about ourselves.

Mr./Ms. ----------.... (one paragraph)

Mr./Ms. ----------.... (one paragraph)

(Other information)

Best wishes from us for a spectacular year!

(Signatures)

ELEMENTARY EXAMPLE

Dear Student,

Welcome to a new school year! We are thrilled to have you as our student!

You may not have had a class shared by two teachers before. This is called co-teaching. Most of the time, we will be in the room together. You can come to either one of us at any time for help.

We would like to tell you a little about ourselves.

I (Mrs. Peery) have been a teacher for thirty-two years. I love reading! It's my favorite thing to do in school or at home. I have four pets (two dogs and two cats). My husband and I love spending time with our animals and out on our boat.

I (Mr. Clemons) have been a teacher for five years. I love being in the outdoors. I also enjoy deep-sea fishing. I have a wife, two dogs, and a newborn baby at my house!

We both want you to do your very best this year and are here to support you.

Best wishes from us for a spectacular year,

Mrs. Angela Peery

Mr. Tim Clemons

SECONDARY EXAMPLE

Dear Student,

Welcome to a new school year! We are thrilled to have you as a student in our ninth-grade English class.

You may not have been in a class shared by two teachers before. This is called co-teaching. Most of the time, we will be in the room together. You can come to either one of us at any time for help. Sometimes we'll teach a lesson together. At other times, we may be working with different groups. There are many ways for us to co-teach, and we hope you'll enjoy having two teachers instead of just one for this class.

We would like to tell you a little about ourselves.

I (Mrs. Peery) have been a teacher for thirty-two years. My teaching certification is English. I love reading and writing and have published thirteen books. I currently have four pets (two dogs and two cats). My husband and I live on Lady's Island and love spending time with our animals and out on our boat. On just about any weekend, you can find me taking a boat ride. I also love to cook. Whenever I have spare time, I'm watching cooking shows.

I (Mrs. Merriam) have been a teacher for thirty-six years. My teaching certifications include several areas of special education and also psychology. I live on the north end and love taking walks on the beach. I have one son and two grandchildren, a boy and a girl, who are the light of my life. You will probably hear me talk about my grandkids a lot.

In this class, we will ask you to read books of your choice at all times. That is the main reading requirement. You'll write at least two essays per quarter, in addition to all sorts of writing of your choice. We'll work on reading and writing in a workshop format; you'll learn more about that very soon. We will also read *Romeo and Juliet* this year (it's one of Mrs. Peery's favorite things to teach). There will be some traditional tests in this class, but much of the work is your independent reading and your writing things you choose to write.

Best wishes from us for a spectacular year,

Mrs. Angela Peery

Mrs. Sandie Merriam

---

online resources This resource can be found at http://resources.corwin.com/coteachersplaybook

Elementary

Dear Parent or Guardian,

We are thrilled to have _ _ _ _ _ _ _ in our co-taught _ _ _ _ _ _ _ grade class this year! We would like to introduce ourselves to you and tell you a little bit about what we will be doing and learning.

Mr. X has been an educator for _ _ _ _ _ _ _ years. He has been part of _ _ _ _ _ _ _ School for _ _ _ _ _ _ _ years and is looking forward to getting to know your _ _ _ _ _ _ _ (student) very well.

Ms. Y has been an educator for _ _ _ _ _ _ _ years. She has been here at _ _ _ _ _ _ _ School for _ _ _ _ _ _ _ years and can't wait to work with your child!

Our class is co-taught by the two of us. That means we are both responsible for planning, teaching, and grading. Some of the most important things to remember about our class are as follows: _

Please call or e-mail us at any time. We look forward to a successful school year.

(Both signatures)

EXAMPLE

Dear Parent or Guardian,

We are thrilled to have Kesha in our co-taught fourth-grade class this year! We would like to introduce ourselves to you and tell you a little bit about what we will be doing and learning.

Mr. Smith has been an educator for ten years. He has been part of XYZ School for five years and is looking forward to getting to know your Kesha very well.

Ms. Binkley has been an educator for twenty-five years. She has been here at XYZ School for all twenty-five years! She can't wait to work with your student this year!

Our class is co-taught by the two of us. That means we are both responsible for planning, teaching, and grading. Some of the most important things to remember about our class are as follows:

- Students need to read for at least ten minutes every weeknight. Please read to or with your child if possible. We go to the library at least once a week, so your child should always have a book that he or she likes.

- We assign homework only about once a week, usually in math. Please ask your student if he or she has a math sheet to work on.

- We use personal spelling lists and dictionaries, so there are no lists of words to study.

- You will hear from us in a note home, an e-mail, or a phone call if we have any concerns.

Please don't hesitate to call or e-mail us at any time. We look forward to a successful school year.

James Smith

Rene Binkley

 This resource can be found at http://resources.corwin.com/coteachersplaybook

Secondary

Dear Parent or Guardian,

We are thrilled to have _____ in our co-taught class this year! We would like to introduce ourselves to you and tell you a little bit about what we will be doing in class.

Mr. X is a _____ teacher and has been an educator for _____ years. He has been part of _____ School for _____ years and is looking forward to getting to know your _____ (student) very well.

Ms. Y is a _____ teacher and has been an educator for _____ years. She has been here at _____ School for _____ years and can't wait to work with your student this year!

Our class is co-taught by the two of us. That means we are both responsible for planning, teaching, and assessing learning. Some of the most important things to remember about our class are as follows: _____

Please don't hesitate to call or e-mail us at any time. We look forward to a successful school year.

(Signatures)

EXAMPLE

Dear Parent or Guardian,

We are thrilled to have Cody in our co-taught class this year! We would like to introduce ourselves to you and tell you a little bit about what we will be doing in class.

Mrs. Peery is an English language arts teacher and has been an educator for thirty-two years. She has been part of ABC High School for five years and is looking forward to getting to know your Cody very well.

Mrs. Merriam is a special education/LD teacher and has been an educator for thirty-five years. She has been here at ABC High School for nine years and can't wait to work with Cody this year!

Our class is co-taught by the two of us. That means we are both responsible for planning, teaching, and assessing learning. Some of the most important things to remember about our English class are as follows:

- Students are to read books of their choice at least twice a week for twenty minutes each time for homework.

- Students are always working on pieces of writing of their choice. We ask that they spend about forty minutes a week working on writing as homework.

- We don't usually send the textbook home. However, we have a class set in our room that we use when we need to. The textbook issued to your student can remain at home or in his/her locker.

- We give students a calendar each month that shows what we're doing in class each day.

- We will go on a field trip in the spring to see a Shakespearean play. More details will be shared at a later date.

Please don't hesitate to call or e-mail us at any time. We look forward to a successful school year.

Angela Peery

Sandie Merriam

---

online resources This resource can be found at http://resources.corwin.com/coteachersplaybook

Extension 1 Co-Teaching Scavenger Hunt

This activity can be done at any time early in the school year when you and your co-teaching partner have about an hour to meet. Ideally you would complete the task together and discuss it all along the way. You may want to assemble these materials into a shared folder, online notebook, or master document to reference for the remainder of the year.

1. Find your school system's mission and vision statements. (Discuss how these apply to your work.)

2. Find your school's mission and vision statements. (Discuss how you will make them come alive in your co-taught classroom.)

3. Make sure you have copies of your school's floor plan and master schedule.

4. What is your school or district's homework policy and grading scale?

5. Where/how can both of you quickly find the phone numbers and e-mail addresses of parents you'll need to reach?

Extension 2   Create a Co-Teaching Vision Board

This could be a fun way to spend an hour after school one day. Put on a pot of coffee or grab your beverage of choice, have some snacks, and dig in! You can work alone or with your co-teaching partner, or you can create an online version of your vision board together on Pinterest!

What is a vision board? A vision board (or inspiration board) is a visualization tool that you can use as inspiration; in this case, it should be a representation of your vision and dreams for your school year. The board should be a collage of pictures, words, quotes, and decoration that reminds you of your passion and purpose in educating the youngsters in your care.

Supplies:

> Computer with Internet access and a color printer
>
> Magazines and wall calendars (bring your own or ask the art teacher if he/she has any to spare)
>
> Newspapers (if there are some handy)
>
> Markers, paint pens, stenciling tools
>
> Posterboard, foam board, cork board, or framed/stretched canvas
>
> Glue sticks or rubber cement
>
> Scissors and/or X-Acto knives
>
> Straight pins or thumb tacks

Process:

1. Ensure you won't be disturbed. Put a "do not disturb" sign on the classroom door. Set your cell phone to silent.

2. Play some music to get you into the mood. You may want to play soothing music, or you may want to play something peppy and upbeat.

3. Think about what you want to manifest in your teaching. How do you want to feel? What do you want to impart? What kind of atmosphere do you want to create? You may want to write about these questions before you start creating the board itself.

4. Start looking for words and images that align with your vision. Cut them out.

5. Place the words and images on your board. Move them around and pin or tack them until you find the arrangement you want.

6. Glue the words and images down when you have settled on the arrangement you want. Decorate with markers, paint pens, etc. as you wish. You may want to write favorite words, phrases, or quotations on the board.

7. Display your finished board in your classroom if you wish.

online resources This resource can be found at http://resources.corwin.com/coteachersplaybook

RELATING

Introduction

Both researchers and practitioners have ample advice about how to co-teach effectively, and as a person who has been in the trenches as a co-teacher myself, so do I. I will not bore you with all the citations and specifics here but instead will get right to the core of the matter. One point is very clear in all the research and in every conversation that I've been involved in as a co-teacher, administrator, researcher, and consultant: **The relationship between the co-teachers is the most important determinant of the success of the team.** I'll say it again more concisely: The relationship between co-teachers is the number one thing to be concerned about! Without a successful partnership between the adults, students will not achieve their full potential. So, it behooves all who are co-teaching partners to devote time and effort to developing and sustaining a good working relationship.

> *"The relationship between the co-teachers is the most important determinant of the success of the team."*

First, however, it may be beneficial to take a brief look inward. Let's start with your assessment of your own strengths. Complete the next activity and share with your co-teaching partner. Discuss how your strengths complement each other and how your differences can be advantageous when serving your students.

Activity: What I Bring to the Table

Check what you deem to be your best qualities. Choose all the words and phrases that people use to describe you and that you could use to describe yourself.

_____ Punctual	_____ Generous
_____ Organized	_____ Resourceful
_____ Serious	_____ Loyal
_____ Analytical thinker	_____ Ethical
_____ Global thinker	_____ Task-oriented
_____ Easygoing	_____ Empathetic
_____ Friendly	_____ Caring
_____ Introverted	_____ Reliable
_____ Extroverted	_____ Carefree
_____ Flexible	_____ Spontaneous
_____ Creature of habit	_____ Slow and steady
_____ Passionate	_____ Fast and furious
_____ Scholarly	_____ Out-of-the-box thinker
_____ Practical	_____ Problem-solver
_____ Creative	_____ Good leader
_____ Logical	_____ Good teammate

After completing this checklist, how do you feel? What qualities are you most proud of?

After sharing your answers with your co-teaching partner, reflect upon these questions:

What strengths do you and your partner share? In other words, how are the two of you alike? How can these similarities be leveraged for student success?

In what areas do you and your co-teaching partner differ? How can these differences be leveraged for student success?

The Four Pillars of a Great Co-Teaching Partnership

The last twenty years of research, scholarly writing, informal writing, and anecdotal evidence about co-teaching point to several overarching characteristics of an effective partnership, which I will call the four pillars for the remainder of this book. The four pillars are the following:

1. Respect

2. Communication

3. Flexibility

4. Humor

Co-teaching partners need to be aware of and work on each of these four pillars at all times. Similar to a good marriage, attention must be paid to several qualities of the relationship at all times or the relationship will suffer—arguments will ensue, you may feel uncomfortable being in the same room together, and the kids will notice. You just can't hide relationship problems from your students. So, commit to yourself and commit to your co-teaching partner. Make a promise to work on these four components of your relationship, and everything will go much more smoothly than if you didn't.

Briefly, let's examine each pillar. Within each description that follows, you'll see reflective questions and short assessment activities you may choose to do while you're reading or after you're finished. Additionally, at the end of this chapter, you'll find bonus materials related to the four pillars and reproducibles you can use throughout the school year.

Pillar 1: Respect

Not surprisingly, mutual respect is the foundation upon which to build the co-teaching alliance. The two teachers spend much of their time facing students together, watching each other work—watching each other soar, thrive, stumble, and fall. Most teachers feel quite vulnerable when another adult watches them teach; perhaps this is an outgrowth of the American model of teaching, which doesn't often require peers to observe each other except in cursory ways. Many experienced teachers have also taught alone for years and are not accustomed to having someone in the room with them for the bulk of the teaching time. Two people simply cannot work in close conditions if they don't respect each other and if they don't put some elbow grease into maintaining a respectful relationship.

Sometimes you'll disagree with your partner, and that's to be expected. As experienced co-teacher and ELL specialist Melissa Eddington says, it's fine to disagree with someone's ideas, but don't make the disagreement about the person. (That's good advice outside of teaching, too.)

Teachers in co-teaching situations that don't work well often report feeling disrespected. Anna Gutierrez (pseudonym) is an ELL specialist paired with a social studies teacher in middle school. When they collaborate, Anna feels her suggestions for tweaking whole-class lessons are not taken seriously by her partner. "She respects me as a professional," Anna stated in an interview with me, speaking of her co-teacher. "But I think because I'm not experienced in her content, she doesn't see my input as valuable."

This is one of the most common challenges I encounter in secondary schools: The content-area teacher devalues or disregards the ideas of the specialist. The specialist may bring this to the content-area teacher's attention, or he or she may not because conversations about situations like these are uncomfortable. If left unresolved, however, a situation like Anna's deteriorates over time. Even if the content-area teacher is not intentionally being disrespectful, never accepting or embracing suggestions from the specialist is inhospitable at best, unprofessional in the long run, and detrimental to the success of students either way. Let's look at some examples of how the lack of respect can derail a co-teaching partnership.

Shannon Sellers (pseudonym), who is licensed in both secondary science and learning disabilities, works with two physical science teachers and one biology teacher at a large high school in the Midwest. The physical science teachers welcome her ideas and eagerly adjust their lessons based on her suggestions. This team of three meets at least once weekly to examine student progress and adjust their upcoming lessons accordingly. They are seeing a steady increase of students mastering the required standards in the classes that Shannon supports. The biology teacher, however, dismisses many of Shannon's ideas and accuses her of "dumbing down" his content. Shannon feels disrespected and finds it hard to even be in the room with the biology teacher because he constantly positions himself as "the expert" and places her in a subordinate role. He allows Shannon to do only menial tasks in his classroom, such as handing out materials, monitoring hall passes, and helping only the students who are part of her caseload with biology content. Once, when Shannon suggested a specific note-taking format and began to model it for the entire class, the biology teacher reminded students that he had previously taught them how to take notes in his class and gave her another task so that she would stop showing students this alternative method.

A team of four kindergarten teachers (who work side by side as two co-teaching pairs) had relationship problems because one of the four, whom I'll call Cheryl, voiced her frustrations to the two teachers who were not paired with her. In some cases, Cheryl also took her concerns to the principal, who then looped in the forgotten team member (Cheryl's partner). The co-teacher who was the last to find out that anything was wrong felt disrespected by Cheryl, and wasn't she right? She was the co-teaching partner *in the same classroom* and was the last to know there was an issue! The team members of the other co-teaching pair felt conflicted and also disrespected by Cheryl, and they worried about their colleague who was unaware of what was being taken down the hall to the principal. How did this group of four learn to work together more effectively? They decided to create a set of norms to guide their work with each other in the future. They also created specific protocols that delineated when an issue was to be brought to the principal's attention. They agreed to not take any question, concern, or action item outside the team of four before bringing it to a whole-team meeting first. Without the norms and protocols, they would have continued their cycle of ineffective communication, frustration, and hurt feelings—and forty students would have continued to receive less-than-ideal instruction.

Words and gestures speak volumes. Respect can be nurtured or injured in a matter of minutes by seemingly innocuous actions. Repeated slights can accumulate until there is a huge obstruction. Cultivating and maintaining respect for your co-teaching partner is priority number one.

Activity: Reflect and Write

Consider the varied definitions of the word *respect* below.

From Merriam Webster online (https://www.merriam-webster.com):

Respect (n.) –

1. high or special regard: esteem

2. the quality or state of being esteemed

From Dictionary.com:

Respect (n.) –

Esteem for or a sense of the worth or excellence of a person, a personal quality, or ability, or something considered as a manifestation of a personal quality or ability.

From the Cambridge Dictionary online (https://dictionary.cambridge.org/us):

Respect (n.) –

Admiration felt or shown for someone or something that you believe has good ideas or qualities.

Which definition resonates most strongly with you right now? Why?

As you know, the word *respect* is not only a noun, it is also a verb. Respect manifests itself in words and actions. Which of the following do you consider to be demonstrations of respect? Check all that apply.

_____ When someone listens to me without distraction.

_____ When someone gives me eye contact as I'm speaking to them.

_____ When someone allows me to speak without interrupting me.

_____ When someone tells me that they respect or value me.

_____ When someone stays out of my personal space.

_____ When someone asks me to help them make a decision.

_____ When someone thanks me.

_____ When someone writes me notes.

_____ When someone brings me small gifts or tokens of appreciation.

_____ When someone spends quality time with me.

-------- When someone plans something special for me.

-------- When someone asks me if they can use or borrow something that belongs to me.

-------- When someone shares their belongings with me.

-------- When someone helps me do something without my asking.

These statements represent actions that occur in schools on a daily basis. They also represent situations in which misunderstandings can occur and feelings can be hurt. For example, I am adamant about people not interrupting a speaker, whomever that speaker is. I spent a great deal of time teaching my students about active listening, and all of us were practitioners of it in my classroom. So imagine how I might feel if I were partnered with a co-teacher who finished my sentences for me if I paused or who jumped into every conversation I was having and started talking when I was talking. To me, those actions are incredibly disrespectful. But for someone who is an active verbal processor, those situations mean nothing. The active verbal processor is talking to learn, to think through things, and has no idea that I'm seething when she speaks over me—unless, of course, I tell her that I consider interruptions disrespectful.

Pillar 2: Communication

Educational consultant and author Anne Beninghof (2012) often asks participants in her workshops about co-teaching to complete the following analogy: "The marriage between special education and general education is like . . . " We could expand this analogy a bit by saying instead, "The marriage between co-teachers is like . . . " I would complete the analogy in this way: The marriage between co-teachers is like a practiced and carefully orchestrated waltz. Both partners have to be in sync with each other for the dance to be as beautiful as it can be. If you don't like the term *marriage*, feel free to replace it with *partnership* or another synonym.

Beninghof (2012) shares the following answers, which may be more to your liking than my contribution: "The marriage . . . is like peanut butter and jelly—each good on their own, but better together. . . . The marriage . . . is like being a one-legged man in a butt-kicking contest. The marriage . . . is like a fine wine—it gets better with age. The marriage . . . is like a roller-coaster ride—sometimes thrilling, sometimes making you sick to your stomach" (p. 15).

Perhaps you have not even begun working with your partner. Or perhaps you're already a few months or even a few years into co-teaching. Right now, to what would you compare the relationship? Complete the following:

The marriage/partnership between co-teachers is like ----------------------------

----

When thinking about how to analogize the co-teaching relationship, most of us would certainly think about communication. Effective communication between the co-teaching partners —and effective communication about the co-teaching partnership to others beyond the pair—is at the center of a healthy working relationship.

Co-teaching teams have different methods to create and sustain the communication necessary for their "marriage" to work well. Teachers Melissa Eddington and Jennifer Wolf use the Voxer app throughout the school day and on their drives home to send messages back and forth to each other. Voxer works like a walkie-talkie and allows back-and-forth conversation in real time when two people are not physically close to each other. Some other teams I've worked with use texting and e-mails throughout each day to share updates. Voxer, texts, and e-mails can all work well, especially if one teacher has urgent information or a time-sensitive question about a particular student.

Surely the fact that effective communication is necessary for co-teaching should come as no surprise. Most workplace relationships are heavily influenced by the communication that takes place within the organization as a whole and among individual members of the organization. However, as I've noted previously, many teachers are accustomed to being the only adult in the room conducting lessons. Once you add another teacher into the mix, the climate changes considerably. As Anne Beninghof (2012) notes, we are "mired in a climate of separateness" (p. 16).

Before discussing the particulars of how and when you'll communicate, a co-teaching pair should discuss each person's basic philosophy of education since this can be at the root of many misunderstandings and communication failures. You don't have to write a formal statement (but you can, if you wish to do so, or if you have such a statement from a paper you've written or a project you've done recently). At minimum, think about the questions in the next activity. Write about them as time allows. Then, discuss them with your partner.

Activity: My Beliefs about Teaching

1. What words do you think are synonymous with *teacher*? (For example, *facilitator, coach, mentor, scholar, trainer, expert.*)

    ----

2. What does "good teaching" mean to you? How would you describe it? You may want to think about good teachers you had in your past. What qualities did they exhibit? What did they say or do that helped you learn?

    ----

3. How do you feel that students learn best? What kinds of environments and experiences help them learn?

    ----

4. How do you hope that your former students remember you? What would you like for them to say about you and your teaching?

Effective communication is not only impacted by one's deeply held beliefs, it is also impacted by day-to-day, seemingly mundane interactions. You and your co-teacher will need to communicate frequently, both when you're in the room working together and when you're apart—even in the evenings and on weekends as you plan, grade papers, and reflect on what has been happening at school.

The questions on the following page are the ones I use in workshops with co-teachers as a baseline for communication for the school year. Discuss them with your co-teacher as soon as possible after you become engaged in the partnership.

Activity: Important Questions for Us to Discuss

Discuss the following with your teaching partner. Record any information that you want to ensure you remember.

1. When I need to ask or tell you something as you're teaching, how would you like for me to do that?

   ----

2. When I need to ask or tell you something when we're not together, how would you like for me to do that (e-mail, phone call, text, voice-to-voice app, etc.)? Are any times off limits (dinner time, Sunday afternoons, etc.)? If a matter is urgent, how should I reach out to you?

   ----

3. When someone calls the classroom or comes to the door, how will we handle it? How have you and your students handled these types of disruptions in the past?

   ----

4. How/when/where will we discuss confidential student information?

----

5. What is the one student behavior that absolutely drives you nuts (and how can we handle this together)?

----

6. What is the one thing that I can do to immediately brighten your day when you really need it?

Remember that you and your partner may have very different communication styles and preferences. The best advice I can give here is to remind you that you should aim to communicate in your *partner's* style and using your *partner's* preferences as often as possible in order to get the best results. I learned this not from co-teaching but from marriage. (See how that marriage analogy activity is still pertinent here?) We teachers are often masters of communicating with students, especially the difficult ones, yet we fail to apply the same concepts to our relationships with co-workers or family members.

The most useful communication tips I have learned over the years are provided below. They can be useful not only in your relationship with your co-teacher but also with your other colleagues as well.

First, use "I" messages versus "you" messages. This may be the biggest and best tip of all. A carefully crafted "I" message states what you, the speaker, feels or thinks and does not accuse the other person of anything or shift blame to that person. So, for example, if my co-teacher were often late to my class, I might say, "When you're late, it really affects how well the lesson goes. We don't get off to a good start." A better way to state this, using the "I" message concept, might be, "I feel concerned when you arrive late to class. I'm worried about where you might be, and I don't think I do as good of a job opening the lesson when you're not with me." Focus on your own thoughts and feelings when making "I" statements. Include the data or actions of the other person but focus on *your* thoughts and emotions. This is much less likely to make the other person feel criticized, attacked, or blamed, yet it does let that person know what they contributed. This allows the other person to reflect on and modify their behavior based on how they have made you feel, not just because they feel scolded.

Communication tip #1:
Use "I" messages.

Second, use the skill of mirroring. Basically, mirroring is exactly what it sounds like: One person behaves as much like the other as possible, acting as a direct reflection of sorts of the other. Mirroring can be both verbal and nonverbal. As a school administrator, I often had teachers come into my office noticeably upset. Their body language indicated it—folded arms, furrowed brows, pacing. There were many physical indicators of their stress. Also, they were often speaking quickly and using words that demonstrated their anger, confusion, or concern. Now, certainly at times it was part of my job to calm them down, but in most cases, I could employ some mirroring to start our conversation and to show them I was on their side, that I wanted to hear what they had to say, and that I wanted to support them. So, if a teacher entered my office and stood at my desk with hands on hips or arms folded, I might stand up behind my desk or move toward the teacher and assume a similar stance. If a teacher said, "You've got to do something about this!" I might say, "Yes, I agree, we need to do something about this!" Mimicking or approximating the other person's gestures and using the same or similar words makes that person immediately feel seen, heard, and "in sync" with you in some way. These simple efforts on your part can help the two of you communicate more effectively each time you face a difficult conversation.

Communication tip #2: Mirror the other person's words and gestures.

Third, remember to paraphrase and summarize. (This is the one time when it's best to use "you" statements versus "I" statements!) There are many ways to capture the essence of what your partner is saying, but please don't use the 1970s hippie phrase, "What I hear you saying is . . . " This particular sentence stem is widespread and is often used without the speaker doing any mental work whatsoever except sticking it before a direct repetition of the other person's words. On the other hand, when thoughtfully paraphrasing and summarizing, you are showing that you are giving your undivided attention to the other person. This allows that person to feel both heard and valued.

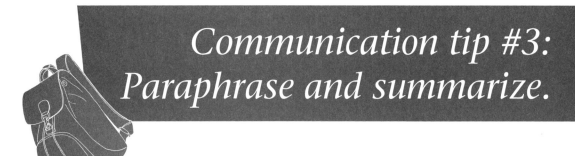

Communication tip #3: Paraphrase and summarize.

Effective ways to paraphrase include using the following sentence stems as you begin talking:

- If I'm understanding you correctly, you said/feel/want . . .

- So you were angry/upset/frustrated/concerned when . . .

- You're thinking . . .

- You're wondering . . .

Effective ways to summarize include:

- Your main points/concerns are . . .

- So there's a difference between _____ and _____

- The theme/pattern that has emerged here is . . .

Vignette: R. K. Smith Middle School in Luling, Louisiana

R. K. Smith Middle School in St. Charles Parish, Louisiana, is staffed by approximately fifty-five teachers and paraprofessionals who are all assigned to at least one co-teaching team. These co-teachers shared with me the following words of advice about being part of such a team:

- Be open and honest and maintain constant contact.

- Always be ready to have each other's back. We both have experienced times when we were not feeling well, but the lesson was already set up and split between us so we needed the other to step in. It was only successful because we both know the curriculum and expectations.

- Feel comfortable to speak with each other about issues privately. Do not gossip about each other around the school.

- Make time to speak with each other about other things *not* involving school. Build a genuine relationship.

- Keep it light-hearted. It is okay to laugh and have fun in the classroom with each other.

- Always support the other. Do not undermine your partner's authority by challenging what he/she said in front of the students. If there is an issue, speak with your partner teacher about it privately or after class.

It's also good to affirm that your paraphrases or summaries are accurate by asking, "Is that correct?" Check in after you've spoken to make sure you've been accurate. However, don't pepper the other person with questions. When seeking to listen carefully and resolve an issue, it's best not to question the speaker excessively. This can agitate an upset person further. Ask only those questions that will move the conversation forward productively.

Lastly, it is necessary to check in with your partner once in a while, even if no problems are begging for attention. Ariel Sacks (2014) reminds us that periodically we simply need to check in with our co-teacher about how we are doing together in general. She recommends asking your partner the following:

- Are there management items we should clarify, such as when are students allowed to go to the bathroom?

- Are we sharing airtime well?

- Are we dividing grading in an equitable way?

- Are there teaching formats that would better utilize the two of us in the classroom?

Co-teaching pairs don't have to discuss questions like the above only when in school and when having meetings together; they also can debrief by having coffee, an adult beverage, or a meal together. Consider establishing a monthly check-in time that occurs away from school and in a place that you both find pleasant. This could be anything from having coffee together to taking a hike in the woods.

Pillar 3: Flexibility

In a personal communication with me, teacher Jennifer Wolf distilled what I consider to be the best advice for co-teachers about flexibility by giving us these reminders: "Be flexible. Be willing to learn from each other. Laugh it off. Don't take yourself too seriously—take the work seriously—but allow yourself failures."

Jennifer's words speak volumes about what goes on in a co-teaching partnership. Because of the culture of separateness that many teachers have come to accept as part and parcel of the job, "being flexible" takes on a new meaning when one is sharing his or her classroom with another adult. When you're the only adult in the room most of the day with your students, "being flexible" means responding to students and adapting to their needs, but it doesn't necessarily mean adjusting to the personality, style, needs, or actions of another adult.

Sometimes self-awareness is part of flexibility. Justin Garcia (2018a) reminds us that "there's only so much you can plan with teaching. Unlike other professions, a lot of what happens in the classroom happens organically. After all, you have a room full of little people with big personalities. I also have a strong personality, and it may come off as domineering or brash. I need to take a step back, breathe, and let loose of control."

In order to help you think about some ways you may need to be flexible when working with a co-teaching partner, complete the next activity.

Activity: My Preferences in the Classroom

Below you'll see pairs of statements that may seem like opposites. Choose the statement in each pair that seems the *most* like you—it doesn't have to be 100% accurate. Later, compare answers with your co-teacher and see where you might differ. Talk with each other about how both of you may need to bend a little bit in areas where you chose different answers.

1a. I believe arriving five minutes early to an appointment is best.	1b. I believe in a fifteen-minute window for any appointment; there are just too many factors that could impede someone.
2a. The allotted time for a class activity or assignment should be strictly adhered to.	2b. The allotted time for a class activity or assignment should be fluid/flexible.
3a. There is "a place for everything, and everything in its place."	3b. Organization is overrated.
4a. My classroom is well organized in terms of supplies, work areas, and furniture arrangement.	4b. My classroom is comfortable and has a home-like feeling.
5a. I prefer a quiet classroom with little movement.	5b. I prefer a noisy classroom with lots of movement.
6a. I usually prefer that students ask me before they leave their seats.	6b. I usually don't mind if students leave their seats without asking me.
7a. I rarely use strategies that require students to walk around the classroom (stand up/hand up/pair up, gallery walk, etc.).	7b. I often use strategies that require students to walk around the classroom (stand up/hand up/pair up, gallery walk, etc.).
8a. I rely on the intriguing qualities of my content to engage my students.	8b. I like to use drama, gestures, facial expressions, and physical expression to engage students.
9a. I rarely use songs, music, or videos to emphasize things or to make instruction more memorable.	9b. I often use songs, music, or videos to emphasize things or to make instruction more memorable.
10a. Assignments that involve technology need to be tightly structured and monitored.	10b. Assignments that involve technology can be loosely structured and monitored.
11a. I believe in clear classroom rules and procedures that are consistently enforced.	11b. I believe in classroom rules and procedures that are fluid/flexible.
12a. I have a few tried-and-true classroom rules and procedures that I will never change.	12b. I would consider changing classroom rules and procedures based on feedback from others.
13a. I mostly stick with tried-and-true assignments and activities that I've done many times before.	13b. I am frequently on the lookout for new assignments and activities.
14a. I prefer to plan my lessons independently.	14b. I prefer to work as part of a collaborative team to plan lessons.
15a. I mostly teach lessons as they were planned.	15b. I frequently adjust lessons in response to student response/reaction.

Understanding the Activity

You may have already figured out the topics and preferences covered in the activity, especially if you took the time to talk about the items with your co-teaching partner.

Numbers 1 and 2 are about timeliness in general and time as a constraint. Some adults are very conscious about time or even have anxiety about possibly being late. Other adults seem to have no sense of time passing at all! And then there are tons of people that lie between these extremes. I'm one of those people who believes that "on time" means five minutes early, and arriving at the agreed-upon time is actually late. If I had a co-teaching partner who was not punctual—or even worse, one who was often a few minutes late—this would be a huge area of potential conflict for me. The point here is not that one point of view or one way of being is better than the other; the point is that as co-teaching partners, you must learn how the other works, and you must learn how to work together, even if your working styles are very different. If you are borderline anxious about timeliness, as I am, and have a partner who doesn't pay much attention to time, then you're headed for big conflict if you don't work some things out ahead of time. For example, I'd be happy to be the person standing at the door, greeting students each class period, because I'm hyped up and ready to go five minutes or more before the starting time. My partner could be doing something that better fits her or his timeliness and working style—perhaps something more flexible or varied than the door-greeting task.

Numbers 3 and 4 are about organization. Again, most people lie on a continuum in organization that ranges from compulsively, rigidly organized to hopelessly messy. A certain level of organization is good in schools as it prevents loss of instructional time and makes transitions between activities go smoothly. However, there are many things that teachers do in the name of organization that just aren't necessary. For example, I have seen teachers with reading areas that have tape marks on the floor to delineate where each large pillow or beanbag chair should be placed. Surely there's a better use of a student's time (like reading) than to have her or him arrange the pillows on the tape marks.

Numbers 5, 6, 7 are about noise level and movement, two things that some teachers have strong preferences about. Similar to the rest of the items in this exercise, there is no right or wrong answer here, but both teachers should seek to find a balance that works for them and also for their students. We all know from experience and from our own families that young children find it harder to remain still than older children; this is simple biology and psychology. Sometimes we impose adult standards of stillness and quiet on our students when those standards are behaviorally and physically impossible for them to meet. On the flip side, we also need to help our students learn to be still, fix their focus, and grow their stamina at times. The key here is to have a good mix of stillness and movement, silence and talking, every day.

Numbers 8, 9, 10 are more about your personal style of teaching. Some folks are more reserved; others are more outlandish or dramatic. Some prefer a tight structure; others take a looser, more hands-off approach. Some like to bring in tons of media and technological resources; others prefer to stick more closely to what's in their head and what's in the textbook or core resource. Again, both ends of the spectrum on these items are simply where you might be, and there is no right or wrong inherent in that. However, what might be interesting for both of you, no matter where you place yourself, would be to explore a bit toward the other end of the continuum. I have done this in my own teaching in the last few years. As a person who always seemed to have a technical difficulty during a presentation, I was decidedly low-tech. I relied mostly on the examples and anecdotes that I could recall and share aloud; I very rarely integrated video. To push myself in that area, I attended a massive and wonderful instruction and technology conference, and I curated a small set of short videos that I could use repeatedly to make certain points—along with keeping all the examples and anecdotes that I previously used in my repertoire. I realized that I could make my points in several ways, and that in some cases, a video clip might resonate with an audience member more than my words could.

Numbers 11 and 12 are about classroom rules and procedures. Notice that there is not an option that says, "I do not believe in having classroom rules and procedures." These items are more about how willing you are to examine when or if changes need to be made. They are also about student input. Surely you have at least one rule or procedure that works well for you if you're an experienced teacher, and, even if you're brand new to the profession, you've most likely found one rule that works well. The point of these items is to think about how or when you may want to reexamine and/or revise rules that are in place and how you might work with your co-teacher in the process.

Numbers 13, 14, and 15 are about planning lessons and assignments. One of the often-cited benefits of having a co-teacher who specializes in English language learning or special education is that the specialist can offer ideas about how to maximize the learning of students who have some needs that differ from the masses. Therefore, some level of collaboration in lesson planning is desirable. The point of these items is to help you gauge what you might both be comfortable with. For example, you may not be comfortable with changing something about a planned lesson as it's unfolding but would be comfortable tweaking it for another class later in the day. Use these items to discuss with your partner how and when collaboration about lesson planning and lesson delivery would work best for you.

Pillar 4: Humor

Humor is a quality that many people prize in themselves, their friends, and their significant others, and it's an important component of an effective co-teaching partnership. Being able to laugh at oneself is necessary for two people to work together in such an intimate setting if they don't want to drive each other completely crazy. Laughter is also a great stress reliever, and thus it should be employed in situations that are tense or frustrating.

Yes, humor is a great quality, but beware—your style of humor may differ from your partner's. In order to understand each other better in this dimension, complete the following activity, ideally together, discussing it as you go along.

Activity: Let's Humor Each Other!

Discuss the following questions and prompts with your co-teaching partner. If you can't complete the activity simultaneously, do it on your own time and come together to share afterwards.

1. Agree or disagree with each of the following statements:

    a. I think I'm a funny person; I can make people laugh easily.
    _ _ _ _ _ agree _ _ _ _ _ disagree

    b. I appreciate humor in others but don't joke around much myself.
    _ _ _ _ _ agree _ _ _ _ _ disagree

    c. Even when alone, I can humor myself with thoughts or memories.
    _ _ _ _ _ agree _ _ _ _ _ disagree

    d. I like to tell funny stories about myself. _ _ _ _ _ agree _ _ _ _ _ disagree

    e. I don't mind if people tease me; I don't usually get embarrassed or upset. _ _ _ _ _ agree _ _ _ _ _disagree

    f. I get my feelings hurt pretty easily if I'm teased.
    _ _ _ _ _ agree _ _ _ _ _ disagree

    g. I sometimes say things that I think are funny even though they might be inappropriate for the situation at hand. _ _ _ _ _ agree _ _ _ _ _ disagree

    h. Sometimes I cover up negative emotions by laughing or joking.
    _ _ _ _ _ agree _ _ _ _ _ disagree

2. Have you ever been hurt by a teacher teasing you, telling a joke, or using sarcasm? If so, describe the incident.

    ----

3. How do you use humor in the classroom?

---

4. What is one thing you would never joke about?

---

5. What else should someone know about your sense of humor?

Humor can be one of the qualities we most like in our mates, and it can also be used to forge a solid friendship. The key is for each co-teacher to understand what's funny to the other. Obviously, racism, sexism, ageism, and hurtful jokes or teasing should never be part of the humor you or your partner are using. If for any reason you find something your partner says in jest offensive, you must immediately address it with him or her, and it may be necessary to involve a direct supervisor. Be sure not to let a hurtful or offensive comment go unnoticed or unaddressed.

Being Prepared for the Highs and the Lows

You and your co-teaching partner should know each other better than you did previously if you have taken part in all the exercises thus far in the book. But even with the best-laid plans and with all the work you've done to share who you are with your partner, there will be times when there is stress. There will be times when conflict will occur. This is simply unavoidable. You can be prepared for such times by agreeing to norms and protocols in advance.

What are norms? Norms are guidelines, standards, or conventions. In work groups, such as a co-teaching pair or team, overall norms should be set about working together, as should norms about conducting meetings. In your classroom, your norms are most likely your classroom rules—they outline the way students interact with each other and with you. Norms for a co-teaching team are similar in that they are the overarching guidelines that govern the relationship and many of the activities that take place routinely.

What are protocols? I like to think of protocols in terms of a flowchart; in other words, a protocol is a set of specific steps or actions that need to be adhered to in certain situations. Protocols are similar to procedures or routines that you have in your classroom. For example, I had a comfy, inviting reading area in my classroom, but it had a specific set of steps that had to be followed to enter it and to remain in it. Students had to have a book in their hands, ready to read, in order to enter the area. While in the area, they had to remain focused on their own book and could not start up conversations with others. They also could not display other off-task behavior. If I observed talking or other nonreading behaviors, I gave the offender one warning. On the second infraction (in the same class period), the student had to leave the area and was not allowed to return to it for one week. Protocols are more granular and detailed than norms.

Examples of Norms for Working Together

I have collected the following norms from various teams and groups I've worked with in the past decade. Feel free to borrow or revise them to fit your situation, but remember, there is power in creating your own norms. It may be best to use these for inspiration but to craft your own norms; those will have a far deeper meaning and impact on the work that you do.

- We will use phrases like "our classroom" and "our students" instead of "my classroom" and "my students."

- We will use both names (a joint signature) when sending e-mails, newsletters, and other communications to parents and families.

- We will not go outside our partnership with our concerns until we first address them with each other.

- We will not have conversations in front of students that would be better had without them present. In other words, we will not confront, negate, or criticize the other teacher within sight or earshot of our students.

- At all times, we will model for our students effective collaboration and respectful dialogue.

- We will turn the discussion over to one another when we feel the other person has more expertise or experience with the topic or situation at hand.

- We will check with the other person before making major changes to a unit, lesson, or activity.

- We will use humor as appropriate to help us work better together but will never use it to put each other down.

- If either of us has a problem or concern with something the other is doing, we will address it with that person and will always offer at least one possible solution.

- We will respect each other's home/work boundaries.

Examples of Norms for Weekly Meetings

I have collected the following meeting norms from groups I've supported and groups I've been part of. Again, they are shared here for inspiration. Create your own norms that work for you.

- We will engage mentally and emotionally during each meeting.

- We will speak honestly, respectfully, and with consideration of the efforts of every person.

- We will take joint responsibility for facilitating and recording notes from meetings.

- We will maintain confidentiality regarding any disagreements or unresolved issues in our meetings.

- We will use our time wisely, starting and ending our meetings on time.

- We will have data and student work samples at each meeting to guide our discussion.

- Each person will complete assigned tasks before the meeting.

- When in doubt, ask a question! Questions are good.

- Topics that do not appear on the agenda will be tabled for discussion outside the meeting.

- We will not use our cell phones during the meeting—no texting, checking e-mails, taking phone calls, etc.

Activity: Write Your Norms

Remember, norms are like ground rules. They serve as overarching guidelines to help you work together effectively.

You may want to write one set of norms for your work in the classroom and another for your meetings. Use the process and questions below to guide the development of all your norms.

1. Without talking to each other, jot down three norms that you feel strongly about. They can be about anything and can be as specific or as general as you wish—anything from "One person should be speaking at a time" to "We will engage fully" or "We will have an agenda for each meeting."

2. After both of you have jotted down three norms, share them. Where is there overlap? On what do you already agree?

3. Examine the norms you have shared in terms of the following:

   - Have we dealt with both the sharing of ideas and the listening/consideration of the other person's ideas?

   - Have we dealt with how we will make decisions together?

   - Have we established a set, sacred meeting time and considered what guidelines we need so that meetings go smoothly?

4. Write and post your norms in a place where you can easily refer to them; this may or may not be in view of students.

5. Determine when you will revisit your norms to see if they need revisions. Most teams review and revise their norms midyear and again at the end of the year.

6. If any norms might need specific protocols to make them work, use the protocol tool found at the end of this chapter.

How to Handle an Uncooperative Co-Teacher

No relationship is perfect. Perhaps through the exercises and discussion in this chapter, you have found ideas to support a good working relationship between you and your co-teaching partner(s). Norms are perhaps one of the most important components of an effective co-teaching relationship, but how should you proceed if norms are violated or, worse yet, if your partner is not willing to engage productively?

First, as uncomfortable as it may be, you must address the situation head on and directly with the other person. Venting to a colleague or going to a supervisor is never a good initial step. Approach the person directly and ask for a meeting. This is done best face-to-face, as e-mails and handwritten notes can be ignored or misinterpreted.

Second, at the meeting, be intentional about using "I" statements. Something similar to the following statements might help you get started:

- I'm glad we have time to meet. I've been feeling like we need some uninterrupted time together.

- I'm feeling that we need time to reconnect.

- I'd like for us to talk about how things have been going.

Third, write down what you agree to at the meeting. Prepare a summary or, at the very least, a list of next steps.

If you request a meeting and feel as if the other teacher is avoiding it, or if he or she doesn't show up, it's probably time to request help from a coach or administrator. Looping a third person in at this point can create more of a sense of urgency or importance about the meeting.

If you don't feel that a meeting—whether between just the two of you or with a third party—would be fruitful, request that a coach or administrator come observe the team in action and provide you with actionable feedback about how things seem to be working. This is something you can do for your own individual growth and reflection. Let your partner know that you are seeking feedback about your teaching and that you've requested observation. If the situation is going badly, surely the observer will be able to see that, and, if warranted, then the observer can help you both (as a team) plan for improvement.

Conclusion

If you and your partner have completed the exercises and discussions in this chapter, then you are well on your way to forging a solid relationship, which is the number one factor in your success! The rest of the book will deal with your main function as a co-teaching team—effective instruction.

Vignette: The Good, the Bad, and the Ugly

Read the account below from an anonymous teacher whose co-teaching experience did not turn out well.

When I first learned that co-teaching in ESL was a trend, I quickly began lobbying for it at the schools I served. While it wasn't a feasible option for the high school, scheduling it in the middle school social studies period would be possible, and my administrators were open to the idea. Two years later, we rolled it out. First, I was excited about serving my English learners in the content areas, but I was especially happy about the individuals they teamed me up with. Both were strong teachers, keen to differentiation and had worked especially well with English learners. While we didn't have any formal training in co-teaching, we had collaborated on other projects and we got along very well. We all felt this would work—at least I did.

However, once the school year rolled out, I soon realized we were unprepared. While there were different issues that made the model ineffective for us, there was one key element lacking and that was formal training.

Friendship Versus Friction

The friendly teacher . . .

This teacher and I got along exceptionally well. There was no friction whatsoever. Whenever I proposed something different from what he usually planned, he agreed and let me implement the strategy with either a small group of ELs, or at times with the entire class. For example, I proposed pre-teaching vocabulary with the entire class and he agreed to let me direct instruction those days. For units and lessons that necessitated background building, he had no problem letting my ELs sit with me in a separate setting. He essentially went along with anything I suggested. Never argued, never pushed back. The only negative was during PLC time. While he was very agreeable when we worked on our own, during PLCs he pretty much collaborated with the rest of his team and I was just an invisible entity in the room.

The confrontational teacher . . .

The other teacher and I started off very well. She was a much more progressive teacher, very strong in her content and an amazing teacher leader. Prior to co-teaching we collaborated very well because we share the same educational philosophy. However, once in her domain, it was clear that she was going to run the show. So long as I didn't try to change any of her plans, we got along just fine. There were a few instances where I pulled out newcomer ELs for background building or for an alternate assignment, but that was rare. Whenever I offered

(Continued)

(Continued)

to direct instruction or implement a strategy that would be helpful to the entire class, she resisted. She once asked if I was questioning her teaching. While she was in fact stronger than my other co-teacher, it was clear that I was there only to serve ELs, but more of an assistant than a co-teacher. The situation in the PLCs was the same. Although no one openly denied access to PLCs, I was never invited, and when I contributed to the conversation, my comments were not valued and my suggestions were not accepted.

The solution in hindsight . . .

I've often heard that personality is the greatest factor in successfully implementing a co-teaching model. However, in our case, the personalities appeared to be a good match, but we were missing crucial pedagogical training. Interestingly enough, the principal that year was new and co-taught with an ESL teacher in another district. If she had been there the year before, perhaps she would have facilitated the planning or would have alerted us to some important conversation about roles and duties.

Bottom line, we were all clueless about our roles, and while we all conducted ourselves professionally in the classroom and students were served well, none of us were satisfied with the model.

Tool 1   Our Goals

Goals are essential for both individuals and teams. This form may be used to set individual, team, and student achievement goals.

First, use the following list to brainstorm and draft each section independently. Then, come together and agree on team goals and student achievement goals that you *both* will work toward.

Goals for my teaching:

1.

2.

3.

Goals for our teaching team:

1.

2.

3.

Student achievement goals:

1.

2.

3.

EXAMPLES

Goals for my teaching:

1. I will be reading a book at all times, just as I ask my students to do.
2. I will not give homework that has no purpose.
3. I will increase my use of rubrics.
4. I will be intentional about teaching content-area vocabulary terms.
5. I will seek student input on my teaching by using periodic surveys.

Goals for our teaching team:

1. We will use at least three co-teaching structures per week.
2. We will meet once a week with data on every student and plan how to respond.
3. We will read one professional book together each semester.
4. We will explore the use of student-led conferences to be held on parent conference nights.
5. We will go to one professional conference together and bring back at least one innovative practice to our co-taught classroom.

Student achievement goals:

1. Each semester we will have 75% or more of our students with a grade of C or above.
2. Our students will pass the state test at a rate of at least 10% higher than last year's class.
3. At least 80% of our students will be able to write an explanatory/informational text that meets or exceeds the proficient score on the state writing rubric.
4. At least 75% of our students will report that we are meeting their needs on a survey of our effectiveness.
5. We will use a pre- and posttest for every unit in social studies and will guarantee that each student scoring below 80% on the pretest will show at least 10% growth on the posttest.

---

online resources This resource can be found at http://resources.corwin.com/coteachersplaybook

Tool 2   Protocols

Protocols are detailed processes to be followed to get certain tasks accomplished. For example, you might follow a protocol at each of your meetings that includes reviewing the norms first, then working through the agenda, and then closing the meeting with some kind of small celebration or with a statement of appreciation for each other.

EXAMPLES

Protocol for making a decision in a meeting:

1. The topic or problem will be presented.

2. Each person will silently brainstorm a list of possible solutions.

3. Teacher A will share his/her top three ideas.

4. Teacher B will share his/her top three ideas (if different from Teacher A).

5. We will narrow the list to two alternatives.

6. Pros and cons will be generated for each alternative.

7. We will agree on which alternative we will use.

8. If we are not able to agree, we will "sleep on it" and meet again the next morning.

9. If we are still not able to agree, we will ask the instructional coach to be our tiebreaker. We will agree to enact the solution the instructional coach selects from our two alternatives.

Protocol for examining student work together:

1. We will each come prepared with student work samples sorted into low, medium, and high (not meeting standard, close to meeting standard, and meeting/exceeding standard).

2. Teacher A will begin by presenting a work sample that meets or exceeds the standard and will describe why. Teacher B will ask clarifying questions but will refrain from presenting his/her own opinions.

3. Teacher B will do the same process as in #2.

4. We will compare to ensure we agree that the two work samples meet or exceed the standard.

5. Teacher A will present a work sample that is close to meeting the standard and will describe why. Teacher B will ask clarifying questions but will refrain from presenting his/her own opinions.

6. Teacher B will do the same process as in #5.

7. The process will continue in this fashion for forty-five minutes.

8. For the last fifteen minutes of the meeting, we will plan next steps based on what we learned during the examination of the work.

---

online resources ↖ This resource can be found at http://resources.corwin.com/coteachersplaybook

Extension 1 Personality Tests

Personality tests can be used to help us more deeply understand ourselves and the people we work with. According to Anne Bogel (2017),

> The more I've learned about personality, the more I've discovered how powerful this knowledge can be. The various personality frameworks . . . are incredible tools for understanding why we do the things we do, why some things come easy while others are difficult, why particular things about our dearest friends drive us crazy, or why we absolutely cannot stand to watch network news or listen to rap music or make small talk without sounding like a blubbering idiot. And personality insights allow us to understand why other people do the things they do, even when (especially when) their thoughts, feelings, and actions in a given situation are profoundly different from our own. (p. 15)

I highly recommend trying one of the personality tests below with your co-teaching partner and discussing the results together. There are free or low-cost options of all of these available online.

MBTI

The Myers–Briggs Type Indicator (MBTI) is a self-reported questionnaire that allows people to indicate their different preferences in how they perceive the world around them, interact with others, and make decisions. The MBTI was created in 1944 and has been used worldwide by individuals and organizations to help people understand themselves better and collaborate more effectively. To find out more and take an online test, go to

https://www.mbtionline.com.

DISC

Like the MBTI, the DiSC profile is a self-reported tool that highlights people's behavioral differences. You answer a series of questions that are intended to provide you with a detailed report of your personality and behavior. Many workplaces use the DiSC profile with their employees and when forming work groups. You can find out more about DiSC at

https://www.discprofile.com/what-is-disc/overview.

CLIFTONSTRENGTHS

The Gallup Organization's CliftonStrengths assessment is another frequently used tool. This online assessment measures your specific order of thirty-four strengths, or what they call "themes of talent." These strengths are what you rely on to build and maintain relationships, think strategically, plan and work, and accomplish goals. You can find out more about this tool and the reports it can yield at https://www.gallupstrengthscenter.com/home/en-us/strengthsfinder.

---

online resources ↗ This resource can be found at http://resources.corwin.com/coteachersplaybook

Extension 2   Learning More about Paraphrasing Skills

Paraphrasing skills are extremely important when you're a part of a long-term working team and when you have to engage in meetings with colleagues. A very useful article, "Skillful Paraphrasing Allows Groups to Examine What Is Being Said," by Robert Garmston and Carolyn McKanders, is good reading. You may want to read and discuss it with your co-teaching partner or with other groups you're part of. You can find it at QR Code 2.1:

QR Code 2.1

To read a QR code, you must have a smartphone or tablet with a camera.

---

online resources ↘ This resource can be found at http://resources.corwin.com/coteachersplaybook

MANAGING

Introduction

It has been said that those who fail to plan are planning to fail. Every experienced teacher knows that planning is a huge part of the job—teachers must deal with everything from how the classroom furniture will be arranged to figuring out how and when parents will be contacted. This chapter will examine planning not only from the perspective of the individual teacher but also from the perspective of a co-teaching pair who must collaborate in order to make the co-taught classroom run as smoothly as possible. This chapter focuses on planning for classroom management; subsequent chapters deal with planning for curriculum and instruction.

Planning for the Learning Environment

Remember that in a co-taught classroom, both teachers share responsibility for planning and delivering instruction, assessing and grading, and managing student behavior. Both teachers also share responsibility for providing differentiation, appropriate support, and accommodations to meet the needs of all students in the class; despite which teacher in the pair is licensed as a special education teacher or language learning specialist, both teachers share the legal (and ethical) responsibility to ensure that specially designed instruction is provided to students who qualify.

Before instruction can take place, though, the room has to be ready for students. Take a moment and sketch your vision of the ideal classroom in the space provided below. Alternatively, you could sketch a classroom that you experienced as a student or a teacher that you felt was a good learning environment. Think about where the teacher's "home base" is. Consider areas for individual work and small-group work. Is there a comfortable place to read? Is there a classroom library? What kind of technology is present? Think about these questions and take a few minutes to sketch what you see in your mind as you envision an ideal learning environment.

Of course, you may work in a school where you do not have everything handy that you envisioned or sketched above. So, what are your next steps? Perhaps you and your co-teaching partner can examine your sketches and see how they compare to the reality you'll have to deal with. Maybe you both would love to have a reading area with comfy cushions and soft lighting. Perhaps you'd like to have a table with stools so that students can convene a collaborative group on a moment's notice. If so, how could you make that vision a reality?

Another issue to discuss as you share your sketches is individual space. Will you two share a desk? Will you each have your own desk or workstation somewhere in the classroom, or, alternatively, will one of you have your main work space in another location? Co-teachers who work with more than one general academic teacher sometimes have a personal desk in a workroom or office and take a cart or backpack with them when they work in other classes. What's most comfortable for your team?

You may have found out about your co-teaching assignment too late to be able to co-create the classroom environment with your partner. If that's the case, don't give up on some of the ideas that are present in your sketch! It's possible that as the year progresses, you and your co-teacher will find that there are goals you have for students that necessitate some rearrangement and redesign. I personally have never left my room the same exact way for an entire year; there are always issues that come up. For instance, one year I decided I wanted my students to have standing peer-writing groups where they would all read their drafts to each other and function similar to an adult creative writing class or writing group. However, there wasn't really an easy way to do this in my classroom. On the days (about once every three weeks) when the writing groups were to meet, I had to rethink how I had my desks arranged and how I had tables placed in my room. Moving the tables to the periphery of the room made it easy for certain groups to get up and move to those tables while a couple of groups remained in the center and simply pulled their desks together. Another year I wanted to have a den-like reading area that would allow students to feel comfortable and cozy as they did the silent reading that I required twice a week for about twenty minutes. I was able to create a reading corner with a yard-sale sofa, an armchair, and big floor pillows. I took two tall wooden bookcases and placed them as sort of barriers to the rest of the room (and of course I filled them with books the students could peruse). I added a couple of small lamps and an artificial ficus tree. Voila! The reading corner became a homey little place in which to read, and students would almost fight each other to get to it first during reading time.

Jennifer Gonzalez (2018) offers some great advice in her blog post "Twelve Ways to Upgrade Your Classroom Design." As she notes, "There are plenty of changes you can make to your classroom—without a lot of money or space—to make it a much better place for students to learn." In this blog post, she gives several tips for reconsidering classroom design, including (for starters) asking your students for their input. You and your co-teacher can start by asking students questions like the following:

- How do you like to learn best most of the time—working alone or working with at least one other person?

- How could we make our classroom more comfortable for you? Please comment on furniture, lighting, and anything else you wish.

- How could we change the walls of our room to better support your learning? Are there things we need to post or remove? What material might be helpful to display?

Gonzalez also urges us to consider reducing the amount of "teacher space" in the room—even removing the teacher desk to free up space. With two teachers present in a co-taught classroom, there is certainly the potential for twice the clutter, an extra (large!) desk, and more. Consider how to make the classroom as student-centered as possible, which may include turning over more of the space to the children.

Advice for Establishing Routines and Procedures

If you've had the good fortune of being assigned to a co-teacher prior to the beginning of the school year, the two of you have time to discuss classroom rules, procedures, and consequences. Even if this is the case, however, the general academic teacher in the pair probably has already established rules that work for her or him—perhaps they're the same rules she or he has used for a while. Those rules might already be displayed on the wall and appear in documents that are ready to go home or that have already been sent. In these situations, the two of you still need to agree on how these rules will be honored and monitored. You also need to agree on the consequences students face for not following rules and procedures.

A teacher's classroom management policy is a very personal thing, and many teachers haven't had to explain their policy to anyone but students; they have never had another adult working alongside them to enact the policy. So, this is an area in which to tread lightly if you're the teacher who is new to a particular classroom. You can start by discussing these questions with your co-teaching partner:

- What are your current classroom rules? How did you come to have these as your rules? Have they worked well for you in the past? Did you recently change any of them? If so, why?

- What procedures should I be aware of? For example, how do students ask for permission to leave their seats or work areas, sharpen pencils, or use the restroom?

- How do you handle violations of the rules and failure to use correct procedures?

- What would you like for me to do if there's a major disruption? How can I be most helpful?

If you have the opportunity to create classroom rules together, consider the following process:

1. Delineate the broad categories within which you want to place the specific rules. For example, *safety*, *respect*, and *personal responsibility*.

2. Brainstorm things that must be covered in each category.

3. Create the exact statements (rules) that you will explicitly teach students and hold them accountable for following.

4. Create the consequences for violating the rules.

One team's process appears below.

Brainstorming:

Safety	Respect	Personal Responsibility
Knowing where everyone is at all times Monitoring who is leaving and entering Use of materials—what things require permission from teacher	Talking with each other Talking with the teacher and other adults Answering/participating in discussion Other people's personal space	Cleaning up your workspace When/how to use the various seating areas Working in groups

Rules:

- Everything has its place (hands, feet, supplies, words).

- Leave things as you found them (or better).

- Use signals (hand raised to answer, one finger for help needed, two fingers for sharpening pencil, three fingers for everything else).

- Use respectful language and accountable talk. (Use the sentence stems displayed in our room when necessary.)

Consequences:

- Verbal reminder/warning

- Time out/change in seating or assignment

- Recess or lunch appointment with one of the teachers

- Phone call or e-mail to parent

- Work with an administrator

In my teaching and administrative experience, special education students have often been the victims of unevenly applied consequences. If you are part of a co-teaching partnership with a special education teacher, he or she probably has vast expertise in helping students feel safe and in helping them self-regulate. Make sure that both of you ensure that your students know the rules and boundaries and understand they will all be treated equally. And most important of all to note, when the learning environment is both safe and rewarding for *all* students, even students who struggle mightily with academic or emotional disabilities can be motivated to change their behaviors if they think the ultimate consequence is temporary removal from the classroom. If you and your co-teacher create a safe yet challenging learning space and apply consequences consistently, students will work hard to remain amongst their peers.

You and your partner should also consider the following chart, which lists tasks one teacher can be engaged in when the other is doing a typical or frequent task. There is absolutely no reason why there should be any downtime for kids when two teachers are in the room conducting instruction! Consider how you can maximize the learning via your actions and the actions of your partner.

If one of you is doing this:	The other can be doing this:
Lecturing	Circulating and monitoring, modeling note-taking for individuals or the whole class, keeping students on task, retrieving supplies as needed
Providing whole-group instruction	Circulating and monitoring, modeling note-taking for individuals or the whole class, keeping students on task, retrieving supplies as needed
Taking attendance	Stating the learning intentions, stating the success criteria, reviewing concepts from the day before, collecting homework, greeting each student
Passing out papers	Reviewing key vocabulary terms, repeating the directions, making gestures that connect with the content of the lesson
Circulating, providing one-on-one support as needed	Convening a small group for intensive support or reteaching/review
Helping a small group	Helping a different small group
Running last-minute copies	Reviewing key vocabulary terms, giving a writing prompt, asking students to verbally summarize recent content, posing questions and allowing think-pair-share
Facilitating sustained silent reading	Reading aloud quietly to a student who is having trouble staying on task, circulating and having one-minute conferences with individual readers, modeling silent reading personally, choosing students to give book talks at the end of the reading period
Facilitating stations or groups	Facilitating different stations or groups
Explaining a new concept	Using manipulatives or realia to demonstrate the content; drawing or writing on the board; making gestures that connect with the content of the lesson; providing synonyms, metaphors, or analogies about the concept
Considering modifications	Considering enrichment/acceleration opportunities

If you and your partner are fortunate enough to be able to plan for the coming school year before it actually begins, I recommend taking some advice from Jennifer Gonzalez (2016) by following these steps from her blog:

- Actually have a plan. Write it down, communicate it, and keep it simple. A few rules and consequences are enough. Jennifer's tip: Cover a little with a lot. My classroom rules were often only three: Take care of yourself. Take care of this place. Take care of each other. Every rule or procedure fell underneath these broad, simple rules.

- Teach your plan. (This means that you and your co-teacher will have to spend time modeling expected behaviors.)

- Enforce the rules by enacting the consequences.

- Don't take it personally. Gonzalez (2016) admits,

> For a lot of teachers, this is easier said than done. I know it was for me. When students misbehaved, I did kind of take it personally. My heart believed that if they respected me, if they cared about me, then they wouldn't talk when I was talking, they wouldn't fool around when they were supposed to be doing something else. It upset me, and I'm sure that showed on my face and in my voice. It added an extra layer of tension and compounded the problem, making the interaction more about the student and me than about the behavior. . . . My tip: Remember, you're not teaching adults; you're teaching kids. Kids are still maturing. Most biologists and psychologists now believe that the frontal lobe of the brain doesn't fully mature until we are in our early twenties. If your students are younger than 20, it's a fair bet that they just can't control all their actions or think rationally at all times. Be kind to them, and be kind to yourself. It's not your fault, and it's not because they don't respect you if they are out of line sometimes.

Procedures, Consequences, and Recognition

Educator Harry Wong has long been a mentor to me in classroom management, and I've used his materials when working with new teachers for over twenty years. This definition from him is useful: "Classroom management refers to all of the things that a teacher does to organize students, space, time, and materials so that instruction in content and student learning can take place" (1998, p. 84). This definition is an older one, but it's one I've relied on for a long time without fail. The bottom line is that as teachers, we must remember that good management is what allows learning to thrive. I have never seen a mismanaged or disorganized classroom in which high levels of engagement and achievement took place.

Obviously, not all students will be able to follow the established procedures at all times. Not all students will be able to comply 100% with the basic rules you and your co-teacher have established for the classroom. Therefore, consistent consequences must be in place for those times when procedures fail and rules are broken.

At the very least, you and your co-teacher will need to agree on the following procedures and enforce consistent consequences for breaking them:

- Entering the classroom/starting the class

- Being recognized to speak

- When to get quiet (as a whole class)

- How to ask to leave the room

- How to ask for help during independent work

- Class dismissal/leaving class

Let's go through each in a little more detail.

1. **Entering the classroom/starting the class.** This may differ across grade levels, but the overall objective is the same: You need to get the students focused on you and engaged in the work of the day as soon as possible. For elementary teachers, entering the room at certain times of the day might involve students being lined up in the hallway beforehand. For secondary teachers, school policy might dictate that students be in their seats by the time the tardy bell rings. Think about where you want students to be and how you want them to show you they are "ready" (whatever "ready" means to you and your partner) when it's time for instruction to begin.

2. **Being recognized to speak.** Most teachers have significant amounts of time each day in which they are directly teaching content or orchestrating discussion; therefore, it's necessary to know when students want to ask a question, answer a question, interject, or participate in another way. Some teachers use a system of raised fingers to signify what the student needs or wants. For example, the index finger raised means "I want to answer" or "I have something to say." Holding up the index and middle fingers together might mean "I need to leave my seat" or something else the teacher has determined, and three fingers (index, middle, and ring fingers) raised might mean "I need to go to the bathroom." Even in classrooms that rely heavily on student-led discussion, Socratic dialogue, inquiry-based methods, or collaborative problem-solving, some sort of signal that means "I want to speak now" is prudent. Explaining and modeling this signal from the very first moments of the school year will ensure that it is learned quickly.

As for consequences for speaking without giving the signal, these might vary based on the type of activity that's going on when the procedure is violated. For instance, if a student is giving a presentation and another student in the audience blurts something out, this could be both embarrassing and discombobulating to the speaker. One of the co-teachers might immediately ask the offending student in that instance to step out into the hall for a minute or two of discussion and counseling. Removing the interrupter can help the student who is speaking to calm down and regain composure. However, for speaking out in teacher-led discussion, perhaps when something is especially interesting or when a true mental "a-ha!" has occurred, the consequence might be milder. One of the co-teachers could say, for example, "Charles, I'll remind you to raise your hand in order to jump in. Raise your hand next time, okay?" If Charles violates the norm again within a few minutes, there may be another reminder, or there may be a more pronounced consequence, such as moving the offender closer to the teacher who's leading the discussion or a request for the student to stay behind a minute or so at dismissal. What the consequences are is not nearly as important as having clearly communicated and enacted consequences.

3. When to get quiet (as a whole class). There are many times in the classroom in which students are working and the noise level rises. It's important for there to be an all-quiet or "attention on me" signal that the teacher uses consistently so that the class will quiet down and focus on whomever is in charge. Many teachers use the raised arm or a countdown system, or both. Other teachers use a chant that the students repeat or chant back to when they hear it. For example, some teachers say, "Class, class, class!" and the students answer with, "Yes, yes, yes!" I know one teacher in Louisiana who uses "Mac and cheese!" to which students say, "Everybody freeze!" and look toward the teacher. Some teachers blink the lights (which works well if students are busily and loudly working in groups). I used to sometimes turn my classroom lights off and just stand by the light switch quietly; it took only a minute for everyone to respond by putting their eyes on me to wait for what might be coming next. Many teachers, myself included, might use a chime to call everyone back to order. There are probably a thousand ways to call for "all eyes on me" and silence.

Again, whatever the signal is, it needs to be used consistently. It won't work if it's only used sometimes and other times you simply raise your voice repeatedly or shush students. You and your co-teacher should agree on the all-quiet signal and both use it whenever necessary.

4. How to ask to leave the room. Of course students will need to use the restroom, get a drink of water, or go to the office from time to time. In most schools, leaving the classroom entails the student having some sort of hall pass or bathroom pass with them in order to be out in the hall without suspicion. Also, in most schools, teachers are required to know where students are and/or to keep a log of who goes where and when. This is for the overall safety of the school. You and your partner should certainly follow whatever the school policies are, but you should also make the system easy on you. Allow students to do some of the work; for example, they can sign a clipboard or on the corner of the dry erase board as they leave and check their name off when they return. That way you can merely glance at the clipboard or board and tell who is where, and when.

What you want to ensure is that you use as little precious teaching/learning time as possible. It doesn't help anyone for you to have lengthy conversations with students when they need to leave the room or to spend your time writing out lengthy passes. Many teachers use laminated hall and bathroom passes. This can save you time. You can quickly write on them with dry erase markers. I've even seen a couple of teachers use a toilet seat as the bathroom pass! The teacher's name and room number were emblazoned on the seat itself. Now surely a student doesn't want to be seen walking around with that kind of pass for very long, so it's up to the student to get his or her business taken care of and reenter class quickly.

Whatever your system is, it needs to enable three things to happen efficiently:

- Permission is granted.

- The student has an object that serves as a legitimate pass.

- There is a record of the when the student leaves and returns.

Work with your co-teacher to implement a procedure that allows the three things above to happen smoothly, and if the procedure doesn't work as well as you'd hoped, then revise it.

5. **How to ask for help during independent work.** Students must often work alone to practice new skills. Sometimes when this is happening, the teacher and/or co-teacher are pulling individuals or small groups for different instruction and may not be readily available to help those that aren't targeted. For times like these, there needs to be an unobtrusive way for individuals to request help, even if the teacher is busy helping others. Some teachers use stackable red, yellow, and green plastic cups to indicate "I need help now" (red), "I need help when you can get to me" (yellow), and "I'm doing fine without help" (green). This can also be accomplished with table tents made from colored laminated paper. I've even worked with some teachers who have small red, green, and yellow flags that a student can display (these might not work well with younger students). There can be a hand signal for a request for help, too, but those are easier to miss if one of you is not circulating at all times. Again, having a system for this is important.

Even if a student doesn't follow the procedure you've established for requesting help, of course you can't refuse to help him or her! You may want to ask the student to demonstrate the correct procedure after helping them or reminding them to do it the next time around.

In some classrooms, or for certain tasks, teachers institute procedures for asking classmates for help before interrupting what the teacher is doing. The system I used for this was called "see three before you see me." During most periods of work in my classroom, this procedure applied. The student needing to ask a question or get help was to first ask three separate classmates before coming to me and interrupting whatever task I was engaged in (usually a conference with another student). I asked the student to bring along the classmates whom she or he had asked for help, then I would proceed to teach a minilesson, provide clarification, or otherwise answer the question that the original student had that none of the four could answer. Often, the four I had just instructed in turn became "experts" on the topic for the rest of the class period or for the next few days. This was my way of doing "see three before you see me," and I have seen other variations over the years. I think that helping students first rely on their peers before coming to you or your co-teacher mirrors what we do in the world outside school and builds interpersonal and collaborative skills. Consider what you might do to build in peer support before students come to you. It will save you time in the long run.

6. **Class dismissal/leaving class.** Many secondary teachers have the policy, "The bell doesn't dismiss you; I dismiss you." Many elementary teachers have specific procedures to follow for lining up or organizing students in some way before leaving the room. Just as with entering class, you're trying to maximize learning time, and thus ending the lesson needs to occur quickly and smoothly. In general, it's probably a good idea here to address both the physical actions students need to take (such as lining up) and the state of the classroom upon dismissal—for example, is trash picked up off the floor? Are materials packed away or ready for whatever happens next in the room?

For students that violate the norms of leaving class repeatedly, you may want to hold them back a couple of times to speak with you as the others leave the room, or you might engage the support of your co-teacher to find alternative ways to address this behavior. Sometimes there's a root cause that can make it difficult for the student to follow your established exiting procedure—for example, extreme anxiety about being late to the next stop, or even a disability, such as hyperactivity. However, with two teacher heads to put together, you can find solutions that work for everyone involved.

I do not recommend punishing an entire class for what a handful of students do, whether that involves incorrectly exiting the classroom or breaking any other procedure you've established. Addressing a student who has not followed a procedure should be just like other management matters—the consequences should be delivered fairly, consistently, and swiftly so as not to interrupt instruction further and certainly never to impede the learning of those not involved.

> *"Addressing a student who has not followed a procedure should be just like other management matters—the consequences should be delivered fairly, consistently, and swiftly so as not to interrupt instruction further and certainly never to impede the learning of those not involved."*

Lastly, there are many times when it's appropriate to offer recognition for students who have been following procedures consistently, for those who have improved in their behaviour, and for those who may be falling short but showing great effort. Just as a reminder about behavior is often best administered as privately as possible, a private gesture or note to recognize a student who is doing well or exerting great effort can be very powerful. Simple statements such as, "I can tell how hard you're trying to concentrate during silent reading time; thank you" can work wonders. If you're not the type to offer verbal praise or recognition very often, set aside about five minutes at the end of your day a couple of times a week and jot two or three notes to students that accomplish the same task. Some templates for you to use are located in the "Tools" section at the end of this chapter.

Determining Who Will Handle What

You have already engaged in activities earlier in this text to help both you and your partner determine what you're most comfortable doing and in what areas your strengths lie. However, you may want to complete the following activity to formally record a division of labor that you agree to in this moment. It would behoove you to review it after the first quarter or semester of the school year to see if it's still working or if certain things need to be adjusted.

Activity: Whose Job Is It?

The chart below delineates major responsibilities. Take time to discuss and complete the chart with your partner. Keep it in a place where you can refer to it frequently. You may want to post a copy in your shared working space.

Task	Are you sharing this responsibility? If so, check here.	If you're not sharing this responsibility, who is responsible? (Is it one of you, or is the responsible party someone else, such as a supervisor?)	Notes and Comments
Taking attendance			
Gathering materials for absent students and/or ensuring students have their makeup work			
Doing the lunch order			
Supervising parent volunteers			

Task	Are you sharing this responsibility? If so, check here.	If you're not sharing this responsibility, who is responsible? (Is it one of you, or is the responsible party someone else, such as a supervisor?)	Notes and Comments
Supervising paraprofessionals			
Decorating classroom bulletin boards			
Decorating hallway bulletin boards or assigned display areas			
Writing daily learning targets and/or agenda on the board			
Making copies the day before they are needed			
Handing out copies during class			
Reminding students of missing assignments			
Holding tutoring hours after school			
Writing/sending the parent newsletter			

Conclusion

It is no secret that effective teachers have classrooms in which routines and procedures are clear. Learning cannot take place in a chaotic environment. Room layout, the handling of supplies, and interactions need to be as efficient as possible. Disruptions and other problems must be anticipated and planned for, and students need to feel validated for meeting or exceeding behavioral expectations. The exercises in this chapter, while not intended to be exhaustive, should help you and your partner establish a classroom management framework that you can embellish as you go.

Tool 1   Student Compact

A compact is an agreement that two or more people, groups, or even countries sign to show they are committed to something or that they agree to something. In this class, we will sign a compact to ensure that we understand and agree about how we will work together this year. Please sign below to show that you understand our classroom rules and procedures and that we have made clear to you how we will support you in your learning.

I, ------------------------------- (print your name), understand the rules and procedures that Mr./Ms. ------------- and Mr./Ms. ------------- have shared with me. I agree to do my best to work with my teachers to uphold the rules and procedures.

We, Mr./Ms. ------------- and Mr./Ms. -------------, agree to do all we can to support ------------- in his/her learning this year.

Signed this ------------- day of ------------- (year).

Tool 2　Positive Notes to Students

Dear -------------------,

I noticed how you are -------------------------------------. Thank you for your effort! I appreciate you!

Dear -------------------,

Today in class, I appreciated how you ---. I just wanted to say thank you.

Dear -------------------,

I'm proud of you for ---. I really enjoy having you as my student.

Dear -------------------,

Thank you for --. I appreciate your hard work and know it will pay off in the long run!

EXAMPLES

Dear Madison,

I noticed how you are using your squishy ball whenever you start to feel anxious in class to keep you from blurting out. Thank you for your effort! I appreciate you!

Dear Aaliyah,

Today in class, I appreciated how you cleaned up around your desk and around our classroom library. I just wanted to say thank you.

Dear Tim,

I'm proud of you for concentrating on your work so hard today during math. I really enjoy having you as my student.

Dear Cody,

Thank you for keeping your group on task today by reminding them of appropriate voice/noise levels. I appreciate your hard work and know it will pay off in the long run for the group project!

---

online resources 🔍 This resource can be found at http://resources.corwin.com/coteachersplaybook

TEACHING

Introduction

As a teacher, there is planning, and then there is more planning! This chapter
focuses on instructional planning—everything from mapping out the big picture
of how various units will unfold throughout the school year to designing how
your co-teaching pair will teach lessons day by day.

Unit Planning

You have set yourself up for success thus far by arranging your co-taught
classroom, developing rules and procedures, delineating teaching responsibilities,
and so much more if you've come this far in the book. Now it is time to get
to your main mission—instructing students well. This means it's time for
unit planning. The unit is the basic structure that most teachers use to design
instruction. It's like an umbrella placed over individual lessons, and it ties them
together topically or thematically. Over the past twenty years, most teachers have
learned about backwards planning as a way to design units.

Please note that if you have units that are already designed for you, as in a district curriculum, it's still a good idea to go through this process yourself. There is no substitute for digging into the standards you're required to teach, unpacking them collaboratively, creating and sequencing learning targets, and determining how the daily lessons will unfold. You should especially consider what co-teaching structures are most appropriate and how they might shift in order to accommodate your teaching style, the content you're teaching, and the needs of the students. If you teach any subject or course that does not have a district-mandated, prewritten curriculum, the discussion of a process to create curriculum could be applied.

BACKWARDS PLANNING

I first learned the basics of backwards planning, which is also called backward design, among other similar terms, in a workshop with Grant Wiggins in the early 1990s. I was a classroom teacher at the time, and a co-teacher, having worked with my special education partners Joan Grimmett and Sandie Merriam for a couple of years. Backwards planning is basically examining the standards you are required to teach and mapping them from the end goal back to the beginning stages or steps so that students will be able to achieve the end. This is the opposite of what many of us were trained to do in college—fill up the time from a beginning point until an end point, like the end of a quarter or semester.

In recent years, backwards planning has become even more detailed, with teachers often being required by their schools or systems to unpack their standards, tease out the essential learnings embedded there, and create a series of learning goals or targets that will get the students to the mastery of the standard in the end.

UNPACKING THE STANDARDS

There are several views on what *unpacking, unwrapping,* or *deconstructing* actually means. Grant Wiggins and Jay McTighe (2012) have long promoted a deep examination and unpacking of standards as part of their Understanding by Design (UBD) curriculum and assessment process. They offer these tips:

- Look at the main verbs within the standards to clarify and highlight the student performance in which content is used. Carefully analyze these verbs to determine their meaning for instruction and assessment.

- Look at the nouns that signal big ideas. A related approach to unpacking standards involves finding important nouns—that is, key concepts, principles, themes, and issues that can be turned into essential questions and understandings.

- Analyze the key adjectives and adverbs to determine valid scoring criteria for rubrics. These qualifiers of the verbs and nouns can provide a useful and efficient way to create rubrics to ensure that assessment is standards based and at the appropriate level of rigor.

Larry Ainsworth (2006) says that unwrapping standards is an analysis of standards and indicators to determine exactly what students need to know and be able to do through a particular context or with a specific topic. The knowledge in the standards is represented by nouns that delineate content and concepts. The skills in the standards are represented by verbs.

Here are three examples of standards that have been deconstructed and the possible learning targets derived from each.

---

1. Determine the main idea of a text and explain how it is supported by key details; summarize the text. (CCSS RI 4.2)

Unpacked:

> *Determine the main idea of an informational text.*

> *Explain how the main idea is supported by key details. (This implies determining which details are key versus which are of lesser importance.)*

> *Summarize an informational text.*

Possible learning targets:

> *I know that the main idea of an informational text is the point the author is trying to make or what the author is trying to teach us about the subject.*

> *I know that the main idea of a text is often stated clearly in a sentence or two.*

> *I can identify key details from the text.*

> *I can use key details from the text to determine the main idea.*

> *I know that a summary contains only the most important details.*

> *I can explain how the key details support the main idea.*

> *I can use details and the main idea to write an accurate summary.*

2. Explain patterns in the number of zeros of the product when multiplying a number by powers of 10, and explain patterns in the placement of the decimal point when a decimal is multiplied or divided by a power of 10. Use whole-number exponents to denote powers of 10. (CCSS 5.NBT.A.2)

Unpacked:

> *Explain patterns using zeros to represent the powers of 10.*

> *Explain patterns in the placement of the decimal point to correspond with the powers of 10 being used to multiply or divide.*

(Continued)

(Continued)

> *Use whole-number exponents to represent powers of 10.*

Possible learning targets:

> *I can accurately multiply and divide whole numbers and decimals by powers of 10.*

> *I can explain the patterns in the number of zeros of a product when multiplying or dividing a whole number or decimal by a power of 10.*

> *I can explain the patterns in the placement of the decimal point when a decimal is multiplied or divided by a power of 10.*

> *I know that every time a number is multiplied by 10, the value of each digit becomes 10 times larger.*

> *I know that a power of 10 represents a base 10-place value position represented by the number of zeros, so that 10^2 represents 100, and so on.*

> *I know that the same patterns for powers of 10 also apply to exponents of powers of 10.*

3. Gather relevant information from multiple print and digital sources, assess the credibility and accuracy of each source, and integrate the information while avoiding plagiarism. (W.CCR.8)

Possible learning targets:

> *I can locate credible, accurate sources for a research project (print and online sources).*

> *I know that there are different ways of citing sources appropriately—for example, MLA style.*

> *I can adapt my online searches to limit the results to the types of sources I need, to narrow a focus, and to use different search engines and databases to find different results.*

I can quote and paraphrase relevant information accurately.

I can integrate information from academic sources correctly and avoid plagiarism.

You'll notice that all the learning targets presented here are in student-friendly language. Sharing these with students in language they can readily understand helps them stay focused on learning versus simply completing a task or engaging in an activity. Also, most teachers order the learning targets for a unit in the order that students are to achieve them—in other words, the targets themselves become building blocks toward eventual mastery of the full standard. Also, the targets become tools that students can use to self-monitor.

Activity: Unpacking the Standards and Creating Learning Targets

Locate the unpacked standards for your grade level or course and discuss them with your co-teaching partner. Often, school district documents include unpacked standards unit by unit. State departments of education often have the unpacked standards available as well. If you cannot locate the unpacked standards for your grade level or course, work with your co-teaching partner to unpack at least two of the standards you will cover in the next unit. Use the template to guide your work.

Full Text of the Standard	Unpacking—Include Skills (Verbs) and Content/Concepts (Nouns)	Learning Targets
1.		
2.		

BIG IDEAS AND ESSENTIAL QUESTIONS

Larry Ainsworth (2006) has defined *big ideas* as what you want students to discover on their own (the main ideas or essential understandings). He also says that a big idea can be an open-ended, enduring idea that may apply to more than one area of study or a student-worded statement derived from a deep understanding of the concepts and skills just studied (2006). He offers these examples of big ideas in elementary mathematics:

- The position of a digit determines its value in a number.

- Estimation comes close to an exact number.

- Numbers can represent different quantities or amounts.

- Fractions represent quantities less than, equal to, or greater than one whole. (2006)

Ainsworth (2006) ties essential questions directly to big ideas by saying that they are guiding questions to focus instruction and assessment and that they will lead students to the discovery of the big ideas. For example, the following essential questions, after being shared with students at the beginning of instruction and after being focused on, would lead students to the big ideas above.

- Why isn't a digit always worth the same amount?

- What is estimation? When and how do we use it?

- What are numbers? How do we use them?

- What is a fraction? What is its relationship to a whole number? (2006)

Wiggins and McTighe take a broader view of big ideas and essential questions. Wiggins (2010) has described big ideas in this way:

> An idea is "big" if it helps us make sense of lots of confusing experiences and seemingly isolated facts. It's like the picture that connects the dots or a simple rule of thumb in a complex field. . . . A big idea is thus a way of seeing better and working smarter, not just a vague notion or another piece of knowledge. It is more like a lens for looking than another object seen; more like a theme than the details of a narrative; more like an active strategy in your favorite sport or reading than a specific skill. It is a theory, not a detail.

McTighe and Wiggins (2013) have offered these seven characteristics of a good essential question:

1. Is open-ended (will not have a single, final, and correct answer)

2. Is thought-provoking and intellectually engaging, often sparking discussion and debate

3. Calls for higher-order thinking (cannot be effectively answered by recall alone)

4. Points toward important, transferable ideas within (and sometimes across) disciplines

5. Raises additional questions

6. Requires support and justification

7. Recurs over time—that is, the question can and should be revisited again and again

Whatever your view of big ideas and essential questions, and whatever experience you have with them, even if it's no experience at all, trying to create them can be an engaging and fruitful task. Let's reexamine the English language arts standard unpacked at the beginning of this chapter.

Full Text of the Standard	Unpacking—Include Skills (Verbs) and Content/Concepts (Nouns)	Learning Targets
Determine the main idea of a text and explain how it is supported by key details; summarize the text. (CCSS RI 4.2)	Determine the main idea of an informational text. Explain how the main idea is supported by key details. (This implies determining which details are key versus which are of lesser importance.) Summarize an informational text.	I know that the main idea of an informational text is the point the author is trying to make or what the author is trying to teach us about the subject. I know that the main idea of a text is often stated clearly in a sentence or two. I can identify key details from the text. I can use key details from the text to determine the main idea. I know that a summary contains only the most important details. I can explain how the key details support the main idea. I can use details and the main idea to write an accurate summary.

Consider the following big ideas and essential questions for this standard:

Big ideas: Key details in an informational text help the reader understand the main idea. Some details are more important than others. An accurate summary of the text can be created by restating the main idea and using the key details while leaving the unimportant details out.

Essential questions: Why should readers understand the structure and organization of informational text? How do readers make sense of and learn from informational text? How can a reader effectively summarize an informational text?

Activity: Big Ideas and Essential Questions

Draft some big ideas and essential questions for at least two of the standards you will teach in an upcoming unit. Use the two standards you previously unpacked or choose two others, ideally from a different subject area than what you chose previously.

Full Text of the Standard	Unpacking	Learning Targets	Big Ideas	Essential Questions
1.				
2.				

Creating the Unit

The process you have applied to the standards you selected for the last two activities is also the process by which you can begin planning an entire unit. Ideally, you and your co-teacher would have time in the spring or summer before a new school year to do some unit planning together. If that is not the case, then perhaps you can both look ahead in the current school year and plan or revise a unit that has already been constructed.

There are several considerations to keep in mind when moving from unpacked standards, learning targets, big ideas, and essential questions to full-blown units that include daily lessons, formative and summative assessments, and the resources you'll need to carry out all your wonderful ideas.

First, you'll need to return to your unpacked standards and examine the level or rigor or cognitive complexity in each. Many teachers use Bloom's Taxonomy (Anderson, Krathwohl, & Bloom, 2001) or Norman Webb's Depth of Knowledge (2005) to tease out the level of rigor or cognitive complexity inherent in a standard. Often, different parts of even the same standard imply various levels of rigor. For example, the words *identify* and *evaluate* may be used in one English language arts standard, but in most cases, they are very different in terms of intellectual difficulty. *Identify* often means that the student simply knows something when he or she sees it, like identifying the setting of a short story. *Evaluate*, however, might denote something far more difficult, like evaluating how the setting of a short story impacts the plot. Of course, the word *identify* can also sometimes mean something far more complex than simple recall. For example, identifying several equally plausible methods of solving a multistep word problem in mathematics is far more difficult than identifying exponents.

Summative Assessment

Summative assessment occurs at the end of a specified period of learning (such as a unit) and is intended to be evaluative, giving students information about what they have learned and how well, and it also often serves as an indicator to parents about a student's progress.

A summative assessment is often a traditional quiz or test, a paper, a project, or a performance, such as a speech or presentation. Teachers use summative assessments to determine achievement, whereas formative assessments are primarily used to change instruction. (Formative assessments are discussed more in depth in the next chapter.)

Now that you've laid out the big picture of the unit, it's time to design the summative assessment that will allow both you and your students to see how well they have mastered the learning targets.

Let's return to a Common Core ELA standard from earlier in the chapter: Determine the main idea of a text and explain how it is supported by key details; summarize the text. (CCSS RI 4.2) The student-friendly learning targets one teacher created from this standard are as follows:

- I know that the main idea of an informational text is the point the author is trying to make or what the author is trying to teach us about the subject.

- I know that the main idea of a text is often stated clearly in a sentence or two.

- I can identify key details from the text.

- I can use key details from the text to determine the main idea.

- I know that a summary contains only the most important details.

- I can explain how the key details support the main idea.

- I can use details and the main idea to write an accurate summary.

When designing a summative assessment, you must ask yourself *what kind* of evidence you need in order to infer mastery and *how much* evidence you need. For example, for this particular standard, will answering questions based on one passage suffice, or would you want students to be presented with more than one passage? How many items about main ideas and key details would convince you that the student has achieved the targets? Which learning targets must have items? In other words, do the first two learning targets require items on the assessment, or are they prerequisite knowledge that a student must understand in order to show mastery of the other five learning targets?

There are several ways to go about designing a summative assessment for this group of learning targets. Two possible assessment designs are outlined below.

Summative Assessment Design 1: One Lengthy Informational Passage	Summative Assessment Design 2: Two Short Informational Passages
1. Read the passage.	1. Read the first passage.
2. What is the main idea of the passage? (multiple choice, one correct answer)	2. What is the main idea of the passage? (multiple choice, one correct answer)
3. Which of the following details supports the main idea that you chose in #2? (multiple choice, several correct answers)	3. State two or three key details that helped you determine the main idea. (constructed response)
	4. Read the second passage.
4. Which of the following details would/would not appear in a summary of this text? (multiple choice, several items)	5. Answer several questions about the main idea and key details. (multiple choice)
5. Write a summary. (constructed response)	6. Write a summary of the second passage. (constructed response)

The two outlines above represent common ways that teachers consider *what kind* of evidence of learning they need and *how much* evidence they need. Option 1 provides less evidence in that it consists of fewer items overall. Option 2 provides more evidence because it has more items total, and it also contains more constructed-response items as opposed to multiple-choice items. A third option would be to make the entire assessment constructed response: The student states the main idea, then lists/explains the key details that support that statement, and, lastly, writes a summary of about a paragraph. Another option would be to have students list details that would appear in a summary versus those that should be omitted.

If time allows, you and your co-teacher should try to design at least one summative assessment together per month. This ensures that both of you are focused on the learning targets and can support students toward their mastery of those targets. Plus, it's just really good practice in assessment design. As teachers, we can always improve in our understanding of how to best assess student learning.

Obviously, you and your partner will also want to discuss options for providing support for students who do not achieve mastery on the summative assessment. What will be done with them so that they can be reassessed later? What will the reassessment look like? Will it be the same assessment, a different form of the assessment, or an alternate assessment, such as a computer-based reading passage?

Daily Lessons

After creating the summative assessment, it's time to map out the daily lessons. Start with the date you plan to give the summative assessment and work backwards to the first day of the unit. Consider each day to be a complete lesson.

Starting with lesson one (day one), determine how content will be parceled out and taught by the two of you. Consider the information in the following chart to help you plan.

For Differentiation for All Students	For Co-Taught Classes with Special Education Students	For Co-Taught Classes with English Learners

• What about this lesson do some students already know or can do?
 	
• What parts of the content have been covered or partially covered previously? What could be de-emphasized?
 	
• What parts of the content are totally new? How will we introduce new material and connect it to what students might already know?
 	
• What higher-order questions can we ask?
 	
• What student interests could be tapped into during this lesson?
 	
• Could we build collaboration and/or flexible grouping into this lesson?
 	
• Could we build individual inquiry into this lesson?
 	
• How many ways can students show evidence of learning? Could we allow choice?
 	
• Are there interdisciplinary connections we could emphasize?
	• What are the most difficult concepts and ideas in this lesson?
	
	• What vocabulary must students know?
	
	    Tier 2: general academic words
	
	    Tier 3: domain-specific terms
	
	• What information will be presented verbally?
	
	• What information will be presented visually?
	
	• How will students take notes? Are there graphic organizers we can use? Can we use color-coding? Can we use mnemonics?
	
	• What behavior concerns can we anticipate? How will we manage them?
	
	• What specific accommodations need to be addressed? How will they be addressed?
	
	• What social, emotional, and/or psychomotor objectives need to be addressed for special needs students?
		• What content needs to be emphasized?
		
		• What specific language in this lesson will be problematic?
		
		• What vocabulary must students know?
		
		    Tier 2: general academic words
		
		    Tier 3: domain-specific terms
		
		• What visual and/or kinesthetic methods could we use to support the learning of the content and vocabulary?
		
		• What strategies will we use to ensure that all ELs participate in the lesson?

A unit planner with space for scoping out daily lessons appears as Tool 1 at the end of this chapter. The main thing to focus on, even if you have a different daily planner you use or a format that your school or district requires you to use, is the co-teaching structures. Think not only about what's most comfortable for you and your partner but also what would best serve the students in each lesson.

Effective Lesson Design

As you plan your daily lessons together, also consider the structure of each lesson not only in terms of co-teaching but in terms of how the brain works. You'll need to consider how to capture the brain's attention as your students enter the room or begin the lesson, how to support increasing independence as they learn and work with new content, and how to close the lesson in a meaningful way that supports memory.

In recent years, many educators have become familiar with what is called the gradual release of responsibility model. The gradual release of responsibility model stipulates that the cognitive work moves from the teacher as a model to joint responsibility of teacher and students to eventual independent practice and application by the student (Pearson & Gallagher, 1983). Teachers often think of this framework as they plan lessons so that they ensure they are modeling first, providing supported/guided practice, and releasing students to the application phase only when ready. With co-teachers, this can be facilitated in more creative ways than if you were teaching alone. The amount of guided practice, along with the grouping patterns used during this phase, can be adjusted to meet individual needs. While some students might be ready to do independent practice and application, others may need to remain in small groups that get differentiated practice. The two teachers can create two groups strategically.

Another concept about lesson design that most teachers are familiar with is the concept of the anticipatory set. As defined by Jennifer Gonzalez (2014) on her website *Cult of Pedagogy*, an anticipatory set is "a brief portion of a lesson given at the very beginning to get students' attention, activate prior knowledge, and prepare them for the day's learning. Also known as advance organizer, hook, or set induction." Many teachers have now combined this idea with something called a bell-ringer or do-now activity, and while they are not the same, they are related concepts. A bell-ringer or do-now activity is a task that students complete upon entering the classroom or beginning the lesson; it is designed to connect to previous learning and to keep students busy as the teacher does tasks like taking attendance. If you're already in the habit of having your students engage in bell-ringers, consider how, with two teachers in the room, this might be reconceived in terms of creating a true anticipatory set.

Also consider closure. It's common for us as teachers to get so busy teaching the lesson and monitoring what students are doing that time seems to slip away quickly. Before you know it, it's time to go to the next class or activity. However, it's important for student memory that we "bookend" the learning with a strong anticipatory set to attune the brain to what is coming next and with a memorable closure that allows the student to encode new knowledge. Strong openings and closings make learning more cohesive for students.

Formative assessment within the type of lesson structure described here is discussed further in the next chapter.

Planning for Ongoing Collaboration

You and your partner must collaborate daily and complete a million seemingly menial tasks together. This is the part of co-teaching that consumes the most time, but it may not be the most vital form of collaboration. The laboring that you engage in together that directly impacts student achievement is the most critical kind of teamwork that you will do. This means pacing out the entire year or course, planning daily lessons, developing both formative and summative assessments, determining grading/evaluating procedures, and using effective instructional strategies to ensure that all students are learning at high levels. In order for this type of multifaceted collaboration to occur frequently and efficiently, several foundational pieces must be in place—namely, norms, protocols, roles, established meeting times, agendas, and a record-keeping system.

NORMS

Norms were discussed in Chapter Two. Remember that norms are established so that teams can achieve their goals. Usually a group's norms can help its members become more thoughtful, productive, and collaborative. They also help a group avoid bogging down or bickering during times of serious work.

Once norms have been established and agreed to by consensus, the entire group, not just the facilitator, must own the norms. In the case of a co-teaching partnership, this should not be too difficult since the core group is a group of two people. However, if there is a paraprofessional working with your team, or if you are a teacher who is partnered with more than one other teacher for co-teaching purposes, the entire group may need to develop norms together. If you haven't done that as a result of reading Chapter Two, please take time to do that now.

How do norms work in practice once they are established and perhaps even written on poster paper and displayed prominently? Obviously, a poster on the wall doesn't guarantee that the norms are anything more than words on paper. Group members must all take responsibility for making sure the norms are respected and enforced. In a co-teaching pair, that means if one person is not observing a norm, the other person must bring this up. I've seen many groups that are creative about addressing a norm violation, but one of the easiest ways is simply to ask, "Are we enacting all of our norms right now?" You could also state, "I feel like we're not operating within our agreed-upon norms right now." A simple question or statement like these almost always turns the attention of the other person back to the work.

Activity: Reflection Questions

Think about a time in your past when you were part of a group that created norms. Did you feel invested in the norms, as if you "owned" them? Why or why not?

Have you been part of a team or group that violated or ignored its norms? If yes, what happened? Looking back on this, how do you feel? What would have been the best way to handle the situation?

How will you and your co-teaching partner(s) monitor the norms you have established? Can you—or will you—involve others in helping you monitor and revise your norms?

PROTOCOLS

You may remember from Chapter Two that protocols are specific steps to follow in a certain situation. They are detailed and help break down a complicated task into manageable pieces. They also create consistency in how things are handled.

For your co-teaching team to have productive meetings, and for work to be done efficiently between meetings, some protocols are necessary.

ROLES

With a group of only two, it might seem unnecessary to have assigned roles for meetings. However, some groups have other members that join them from time to time—perhaps an instructional coach or specialist. And, as mentioned previously, there are co-teaching configurations that may include two generalist teachers and one specialist who serves both. To be prepared for anything that lies ahead, discuss what your roles will be, at the very least, in your weekly meetings. I suggest that one of you assume the facilitator role and the other assume the note-taking/recording role at each meeting. Because there are only two of you (at most meetings), you may choose to alternate roles, with one of you being the facilitator one week and the other the next week. Of course, it's perfectly acceptable to keep the same role for a month, a quarter, or even the entire school year if you wish. The two core members of your team (you and your co-teacher) should decide.

The facilitator is responsible for setting the agenda (with input) and leading the discussion. The recorder is responsible for taking notes during the meeting and sharing them with all interested or necessary parties (team members, instructional coaches, data specialists, administrators, etc.).

ESTABLISHED MEETING TIMES

It would behoove you and your teaching partner to establish one regular meeting time per week to examine current student achievement, even though you'll be checking in with each other and possibly have other meetings during the week.

The primary purpose of the regularly established meeting focusing on achievement is to constantly stay on top of how large groups (such as a whole grade level or class) and key individuals (students with disabilities, English learners) are faring. The secondary purpose is to table discipline concerns for another time and to focus solely on teaching and learning in this particular meeting.

This once-weekly meeting might be best organized around the four guiding questions of a professional learning community:

1. What do we want students to learn?

2. How will we know if they have learned it?

3. What will we do if they have not learned it?

4. How will we provide extended learning opportunities for students who have mastered the content? (DuFour & Reeves, 2016)

Taking each of the PLC questions into consideration, your meetings should include discussion of the following:

-   The standards you're teaching and the resulting learning targets that have been created based on those standards

-   Formal and informal assessment methods—how can you be sure that students are meeting or exceeding learning targets?

-   What kinds of differentiation, remediation, and intervention do nonproficient students need?

-   What kinds of differentiation, acceleration, and enrichment do advanced students need?

If you spend time in your meetings discussing topics other than those related to the four guiding questions above, then you are wasting valuable time. Teacher teams that wander from these four focal points find themselves not getting the results they desire. Much of the work of a co-teaching pair should be about supporting all types of learners as they seek to master the learning targets that will eventually lead them to grade-level competence. Surely there is enough to be done with that overarching goal in mind to easily fill the time allotted for a weekly meeting.

Use the chart on the following page to plan for your collaboration meetings and to gauge how you're doing throughout the year. Also, see Appendix D for useful "do not disturb" signs you can use to keep your meetings uninterrupted.

Do's and Don'ts for Co-Teaching Meetings

Do	Don't
Use a "do not disturb" sign or other method to let others know you're meeting.	Allow others to "pop in" to chat or have a snack. Take phone calls from the office; if something is urgent, someone will physically come find you.
Have new student data and/or work samples to reference to support your points and guide the work of the team.	Say things like the following: "I feel like they're doing better." "They seem to be understanding." "They're getting better/worse."
Be on time. (Better yet, be early.)	Show up late or leave early.
Create and follow the agenda.	Add last-minute items to the agenda. Bring up topics that are better handled at another time.
Set and follow time limits.	Complain incessantly about any one topic or idea. Allow one task or topic to consume the entire meeting.
Actively engage. Maintain eye contact and use your listening skills.	Use your cell phone during the meeting.
Keep official minutes. Share these with your principal via e-mail or a shared/public document.	Forget to write important things down. Forget to share with supervisors so that they know what you're doing.
Keep things positive.	Complain about students or colleagues. Complain about having to meet all the time.
Occasionally invite an administrator or instructional coach.	Ask an administrator or instructional coach to come to the meeting to mediate disputes between you and your partner.
End on time. (Better yet, end a couple of minutes early.)	Continue meeting even though students are in the hallway on the way to your room. Continue meeting past the agreed-upon time unless you agreed to it when the meeting started.

AGENDAS

A pre-planned agenda can help each meeting go swiftly and, more importantly, it keeps your team on track in meeting your goals.

You may work in a school or system that has created agenda templates for teams to use. If so, and if these templates are helpful for your co-teaching meetings, then by all means use them. However, co-teaching team meetings may function significantly differently from other teams that meet regularly.

RECORD-KEEPING SYSTEM

You and your partner are doing important work; you should keep a good record of it. This will help if your team is together for multiple years. It also helps you share your successes with others who may be interested, such as your principal or possibly people at the system level who are always looking for data to confirm that co-teaching can be successful for both teachers and students.

Your team meetings can be documented in hard copy, if you like, so that you always have a notebook to pull off the shelf so you can see where you've been and you can show your work to others. Most teams nowadays also want an electronic copy of their work. Consider the online notebook tools below if you're not already using one of them.

GOOGLE DRIVE

Google Drive is one of the most versatile (and virtually ubiquitous) cloud-storage services available. It provides a suite of services including Google Docs for word processing, Google Slides for presentations, and Google Sheets for spreadsheets.

Google Drive and Google Classroom are used by many teachers across the globe. The key to housing your documents in a shared Google folder in your Google Drive is to organize well. Your school may already have a system of team folders or team drives set up; if that's the case, work within this structure. If an overarching structure doesn't exist, then create folders for you and your partner to use. I would suggest a folder called "Meetings" and another called "Curriculum" as a bare minimum. Each collaboration meeting that you have could be captured in a single document and saved in the "Meetings" folder. All work related to curriculum, instruction, and assessment (like unit plans and daily lesson plans) could be housed in the "Curriculum" folder. These folders could be shared only between you and your co-teaching partner(s), not made public or shared with the entire faculty.

MICROSOFT ONENOTE

OneNote is a program for information gathering/recording and collaboration among users. It gathers many forms of notes, drawings, screen clips, and audio. When you create a OneNote notebook, it can be shared with other users.

In OneNote, you can create text, tables, pictures, and drawings, much like in Microsoft Word. However, unlike word processing programs, OneNote has windows that have fewer restrictions about what you can do. For example, you can create a new text box anywhere. Also, OneNote saves your work automatically.

OneNote saves information in pages, sections, and notebooks, much like hard copy. The overarching design is like a tabbed binder, which is a comfortable interface for both teachers and students. You can gather notes and materials from other applications and websites. There is no set page layout or structure, and your files can be really large if you like.

Evernote and OneNote are very similar; they are both cloud-based notebooks. Evernote differs from OneNote a bit in its tagging capabilities; Evernote allows you to create custom tags, whereas OneNote limits what you can create as notebook sections. With Evernote, you can gather notes and materials from other applications and websites.

LIVEBINDERS

This is an Internet-based binder/notebook system; you do not need to have the program on your computer in order to use it. It is free and online. You can create a binder that will gather your documents, websites, links, etc. all in one place.

OneNote, Evernote, and LiveBinders are terrific options for teachers who are new to cloud-based storage and would like to create something that is like a real-life three-ring binder with sections, tabs, and pages. Each of these notebook-type options may also be preferable for teachers who find shared Google drives and folders confusing or cumbersome.

Tips for Calendaring Meetings

Without planning ahead, you won't hold all your meetings. It is absolutely necessary to meet once a week to discuss student progress toward the most important academic goals that you and your co-teacher have established.

First, look at your school calendar. If possible, set a day of the week that will be your sacred meeting day. Of course, there will be some weeks that this particular day is not a normal day—for example, there are school holidays, assemblies, teacher professional development days, school picture days, and so on. However, if you can commit to the same day every week, for just about an hour, you will be far ahead of the game.

Ideally, you and your partner should meet during the school day; however, with the demands on teachers' schedules, this can't always happen. Have you exhausted all the possibilities for scheduling an hour-long meeting during the day? Would any of the options below be feasible?

- Meet when students are in physical education, music, or art class

- Meet when students are in the library

- Utilize a parent volunteer to conduct class during your meeting

- Ask an administrator or instructional coach to cover your class

- Combine thirty minutes of physical education, music, or art class with a thirty-minute library visit

- Meet during lunch (thirty minutes) two days in a row

If you have an hour of open time during the day, such as a planning period, try to utilize it for this purpose once a week. If you don't have this time available, breakfast meetings, lunch meetings, and after-school meetings are the options you have. Perhaps you could rotate these options: one week, meet an hour before school; the next week, meet an hour after school. Be creative!

If possible, sit down together during the first week of school and calendar your meetings for the entire year. Put these on an official school calendar (if one exists) so that others will know how important your meetings are and so that there is less likelihood that the meetings are interrupted.

Conclusion

Planning units, with their embedded lessons and assessments, is perhaps the most critical thing you do as a teacher. The backward design process can be endlessly fruitful for you and your co-teaching partner as you navigate the journey of co-teaching with the goal that your students will experience the most engaging instruction and their highest achievement ever.

Additionally, the ongoing collaboration that you and your partner have based on the instructional plans you've created is vital. If you do not regularly meet to discuss how instruction can be adjusted, students will not achieve at high levels. Planning instruction is one thing; monitoring and adjusting that instruction is quite another, and with the groundwork laid in this chapter, you should be ready to meet the challenges head on.

Tool 1   Unit Plan Template

Name of unit:

Attach all assessments to this unit planner.

Essential questions and big ideas:

Focus standards:

1.

2.

3.

Unwrapped standards:

Skills	Content	Key Vocabulary

Supporting standards:

1.

2.

3.

Student-friendly learning targets:

1.

2.

3.

4.

5.

Daily lesson sequence:

Day	Co-Teaching Structure	Detailed Plans	Resources and Materials
1.	☐ One teach/one observe ☐ One teach/one assist ☐ Parallel teaching ☐ Station teaching ☐ Alternative teaching ☐ Team teaching		
2.	☐ One teach/one observe ☐ One teach/one assist ☐ Parallel teaching ☐ Station teaching ☐ Alternative teaching ☐ Team teaching		
3.	☐ One teach/one observe ☐ One teach/one assist ☐ Parallel teaching ☐ Station teaching ☐ Alternative teaching ☐ Team teaching		
4.	☐ One teach/one observe ☐ One teach/one assist ☐ Parallel teaching ☐ Station teaching ☐ Alternative teaching ☐ Team teaching		
5.	☐ One teach/one observe ☐ One teach/one assist ☐ Parallel teaching ☐ Station teaching ☐ Alternative teaching ☐ Team teaching		

Day	Co-Teaching Structure	Detailed Plans	Resources and Materials
6.	☐ One teach/one observe ☐ One teach/one assist ☐ Parallel teaching ☐ Station teaching ☐ Alternative teaching ☐ Team teaching		
7.	☐ One teach/one observe ☐ One teach/one assist ☐ Parallel teaching ☐ Station teaching ☐ Alternative teaching ☐ Team teaching		
8.	☐ One teach/one observe ☐ One teach/one assist ☐ Parallel teaching ☐ Station teaching ☐ Alternative teaching ☐ Team teaching		
9.	☐ One teach/one observe ☐ One teach/one assist ☐ Parallel teaching ☐ Station teaching ☐ Alternative teaching ☐ Team teaching		
10.	☐ One teach/one observe ☐ One teach/one assist ☐ Parallel teaching ☐ Station teaching ☐ Alternative teaching ☐ Team teaching		

online resources ⏷ This resource can be found at http://resources.corwin.com/coteachersplaybook

AGENDA 1

Date:

Names of those attending:

Purpose(s) of meeting:

Meeting notes:

Next steps:

EXAMPLE 1

Date: Aug. 23, 2018

Names of those attending: Pattie M. (teacher), Sandra R. (teacher), Amy G. (instructional facilitator)

Purpose(s) of meeting:

- To continue unpacking grade four math standards for Unit 2

- Create big ideas, essential questions for Unit 2

- Start designing end-of-unit summative assessment

Meeting notes:

- All standards for both units 1 and 2 are unpacked and are located in the shared folder labeled "Unpacked Standards."

- Unit 2 big ideas and essential questions are drafted and are located in the shared folder labeled "Unit 2."

- We drafted the sections needed for the summative assessment.

Next steps:

- Each team member is to come to the next meeting with three possible items for the summative assessment.

- The meeting is set for Aug. 30, 11 a.m., in Amy's office.

AGENDA 2

Date:

Attendees:

SMART goal(s):

Current data:

Analysis of data:

Notes:

Plan of action:

EXAMPLE 2

Date: Sept. 20, 2018

Attendees: Angela Peery, Sandie Merriam

SMART goals:

At the end of the 2018–2019 school year, 90% of ninth-grade students in Mrs. Peery/Mrs. Merriam's co-taught classes will show at least one year of growth in their reading levels as measured on the ABC Reading Assessment.

Current data:

Instrument was the CDE Reading Drills, Level A. Each student completed two exercises.

Percentage of Students at Mastery or Above	Percentage of Students Close to Mastery	Percentage of Students Needing More Practice
45%	20%	35%

Analysis of data:

- The percentage of students at mastery or above is up 5% from the previous assessment.

- The percentage of students close to mastery is up 10% from the previous assessment.

- We are at 65% percent of students at or close to mastery.

- The number one issue that prevented students from achieving mastery was being able to make valid inferences.

Notes:

We will cover making generalizations, drawing conclusions, making predictions, and using context clues to infer word meaning throughout the next unit. This should help our students do better on inferences when they are assessed.

Plan of action:

- We will meet for thirty minutes tomorrow to discuss ideas for how to teach these skills in a more direct manner throughout the next unit.

- We will meet next week for one hour and devote our meeting time to pacing out the unit and creating the teaching plan for these skills.

- We will give the next formative assessment five weeks from today. By that time, we will have been teaching the inferencing skills for about two weeks.

---

online resources ⏴ This resource can be found at http://resources.corwin.com/coteachersplaybook

General ed teacher: _____   Date: _____

Specialist teacher: _____   Subject/grade: _____

Time: _____

Observer: _____

Brief description of the class and/or activity:

PLANNING

____ Co-teachers have planned the lesson together. (Evidence could include copies of lesson plans or other documents, that materials are ready and both teachers know where they are and how to use them, and/or teachers don't have to check with each other about what to do or when to do it—they move fluidly through the lesson.)

LEARNING ENVIRONMENT

The following structures were observed during the visit:

____ One teach/one observe   ____ One teach/one assist

____ Parallel teaching   ____ Station teaching

____ Team teaching/teaming   ____ Alternative teaching

____ A variety of instructional materials are present to account for the different learning needs of students. (For example, differentiated reading materials, supportive websites ready at computers for students to use as references, posters, bulletin boards, anchor charts.)

____ Routines and procedures are evident. (For example, students know how/when to move into groups, students don't have questions about what to do next, transitions are quick, teachers don't have to spend much time giving directions about tasks.)

‗‗‗‗There is shared ownership of the class; all students interact comfortably with both teachers.

‗‗‗‗Both teachers are observed using high-impact instructional strategies. Check all that apply.

    ‗‗‗‗Similarities and differences (comparisons, metaphors, analogies, sorting, classifying)

    ‗‗‗‗Written summaries

    ‗‗‗‗Effective note-taking, such as Cornell notes, partial outlines, or concept maps

    ‗‗‗‗Focused practice (bell-ringers, working problems, answering questions)

    ‗‗‗‗Graphic organizers (Venn diagram, Thinking Maps, comparison matrix)

    ‗‗‗‗Other nonlinguistic representations (physical models, movement/kinesthetic activity, visualizing, drawing or making symbolic representations)

    ‗‗‗‗Socratic discussion/seminar/circles

    ‗‗‗‗Advance organizers (video clip, short narrative or anecdote, SQ3R)

    ‗‗‗‗Writing across the curriculum (quick write, think-write-pair-share, exit ticket)

    ‗‗‗‗Other (explain):

Record other notes on the back. If possible, sketch a visual that shows grouping(s) of students and movement of both teachers during the lesson.

online resources ⟋ This resource can be found at http://resources.corwin.com/coteachersplaybook

The School Reform Initiative (SRI) is a nonprofit organization serving thousands of educators and students throughout the United States and internationally. According to its website, the initiative's stated mission is "to create transformational learning communities, fiercely committed to educational equity and excellence." You can find a plethora of protocols that may support you in your co-teaching teamwork at https://www.schoolreforminitiative.org/protocols.

The National School Reform Faculty (NSRF) is an organization supporting effective teacher collaboration and school improvement worldwide. Their abundant protocols are housed at https://www.nsrfharmony.org/protocols.

Exploring the various protocols at these two sites has the potential to enrich your teamwork. Enjoy.

 This resource can be found at http://resources.corwin.com/coteachersplaybook

Extension 2   Student Surveys

You may want to survey students about their perceptions of co-teaching. Use or adapt the surveys below.

Early in the year

    1 = disagree

    2 = neutral/not sure

    3 = agree

    ----I am looking forward to having two teachers in this class.

    ----I think that class behavior will be better with two teachers.

    ----I feel comfortable asking for help from either teacher.

    ----I think I will learn more with two teachers than with just one.

    ----I feel that everything about this class has been explained well.

What are you looking forward to in this class?

What are your concerns about this class?

Middle of the year

    1 = disagree

    2 = neutral/not sure

    3 = agree

    ----I am enjoying having two teachers in this class.

    ----I think that class behavior is better with two teachers.

    ----I feel comfortable asking for help from either teacher.

    ----I am learning more with two teachers than with just one.

    ----I feel that everything about this class is going well.

What is going well for you in this class so far?

What are your concerns about this class so far?

What could we do to improve our teaching?

End of the year

    1 = disagree

    2 = neutral/not sure

    3 = agree

    ---- I enjoyed having two teachers in this class.

    ---- I think that class behavior was better with two teachers.

    ---- I was comfortable asking for help from either teacher.

    ---- I learned more with two teachers than with just one.

    ---- I felt that everything about this class went well.

    ---- I would like to have more co-taught classes in the future.

What advice would you give to students in our class next year?

What else would you like for us to know?

---

online resources   This resource can be found at http://resources.corwin.com/coteachersplaybook

ASSESSING

Introduction

A huge part of instructional planning is determining how students will be assessed moment by moment, day by day, lesson by lesson, and unit by unit. This chapter provides ideas for how you and your co-teacher can effectively assess students, focusing mostly on formative assessment.

Assessment in General

Assessment, in terms of what we do as teachers, can be defined as collecting information about what a student knows and can do so that we can adjust instruction to better serve the student or provide a statement about the student's current level of performance. Assessment may be informal or formal. Informal assessment is the "kid-watching" that we do as we teach—observing facial expressions and body language, asking and answering questions, prompting, cueing, listening. Informal assessment also includes a range of tasks that we might orchestrate during a lesson—posing questions, forming groups, having conferences with individual students, asking students to jot down their thoughts. Formal assessment, on the other hand, includes tasks like tests, quizzes, projects, papers, and presentations. These tasks are undertaken with advance notice of what is expected and how they will be scored. Standardized tests, diagnostic tests, and all sorts of screening and benchmarking tools are also considered to be formal assessment measures. In your classroom, there is undoubtedly a mix of informal and formal assessment.

Author and consultant Nicole Vagle (2015) says that high-quality assessment practices do the following:

- Motivate and engage students

- Communicate strengths in terms of learning

- Provide intentional opportunities to learn from mistakes and failure

- Generate confidence and success (p. 1)

In the co-taught classroom, in many cases the general education teacher is the teacher of record who assigns grades for the grade level, subject, or course. However, as argued elsewhere in this book, co-teachers should collaborate in designing curriculum, instruction, and assessment as much as possible. Because assessment practices can always be refined to better serve students, it behooves co-teachers to explore ways to continually improve how they are assessing, both informally and formally. Also, because there are two teachers present in the co-taught classroom, observing and reflecting upon how the assessment process is going should be enhanced. With two sets of eyes and ears comes increased awareness and, potentially, innovation.

Formative versus Summative Assessment

Formative assessment occurs during the learning process and is intended to help the teacher know how to adjust instruction to move each learner forward. With clearly articulated learning goals or targets in place, formative assessment practices allow both teachers and students to understand where a student is at a point in time as she or he is progressing toward the learning targets. Formative assessments are often not graded.

Summative assessment occurs at the end of a specified period of learning and is intended to be evaluative, giving students information about what they have learned and how well. It also often serves as an indicator to parents about a student's progress. Teachers use summative assessments to determine achievement. Summative assessments always include a grade or a score of some sort.

Thinking about Formative Assessment

Many educators would say that formative assessment is the ongoing process and various methods by which they measure student learning day by day, minute by minute, and in both formal and informal ways. Some educators might also say that a formative assessment is a task, such as a quiz, test, or essay, used to gauge student learning along the way to mastery of a standard. Therefore, formative assessment is both a continuing process and a singular event.

What is your personal definition of formative assessment? Use the Frayer model graphic organizer below to capture your ideas.

Define formative assessment.	*Describe formative assessment. What are its critical attributes?*
What are some examples of formative assessment in your classroom?	*What are some nonexamples of formative assessment in your classroom? (For instance, what summative assessments do you use?)*

Source: **Adapted from Frayer et al. (1969).**

Compare your ideas with your co-teaching partner. What are the similarities and differences between your two graphic organizers?

Perhaps my favorite definition of formative assessment comes from scholar and educator James Popham (2008): "Formative assessment is a planned process in which assessment-elicited evidence of students' status is used by teachers to adjust their ongoing instructional procedures or by students to adjust their current learning tactics" (p. 4).

Much of the evidence demonstrating the power of formative assessment was first brought to light by British researchers Paul Black and Dylan Wiliam. They published an exhaustive review of classroom assessment studies drawn from almost 700 research reports. They concluded that the research they summarized showed "conclusively that formative assessment does improve learning"(1998, p. 46). They also pointed out that the student gains in learning brought about by formative assessment were "amongst the largest ever reported for educational interventions" (p. 47). It is also interesting to note that according to their review, there seems to be no "correct" way that the formative assessment process must be employed in order for it to be successful; significant gains arise from many different designs and methods. Because of the power of formative assessment in its many forms, it is worth continual exploration by you and your co-teacher.

Co-teachers should discuss the specifics of how formative assessment plays out in the co-taught classroom. Critical to the definition of formative assessment is that it is nonpunitive; formative assessment tasks are generally not used to determine a student's grade. Instead, they are used to help the teachers plan next steps in instruction. Formative assessment tasks can also, in most cases, be repeated until the student achieves mastery of the learning targets.

The fact that formative assessment tasks are not graded like traditional tasks, and the fact that some students need repeated attempts to be successful, can lead to much confusion regarding how to provide effective feedback to students in the co-taught classroom. If the co-teachers disagree on how to enact the formative assessment process, or if one teacher's formative assessment philosophy differs from the other's, there needs to be a lot of dialogue so that students are not receiving mixed signals.

Activity: Thirty Fun, Formative Assessment Ideas

Examine and discuss the chart on the following page with your co-teaching partner. Which ideas have you tried? Which ideas would you like to try? If possible, choose two or three that you can plan to use within the next couple of weeks.

Create a metaphor or analogy based on our content.	One-word summary: What one word best sums up the lesson and why?	Three most important words: What three words best sum up our lesson or would help you remember the content?	Sketch: Take two minutes to sketch something that will help you remember what we learned today.	Turn and talk: Tell your partner ____.
Plus/delta: What was positive or helped you learn today? What would you change?	Two pluses and a wish: What things were positive or supported you in your learning? What do you wish had been different?	Think-pair-share: Pose a question. Allow think time. Students pair up and share answers.	Think-write-pair-share: Pose a question. Students write (silently) for a minute or two. Students pair up and share answers.	ABC summary: Assign each student a letter of the alphabet. They must come up with a word that starts with that letter and explain how it relates to the content.
Tic-tac-toe board: Display nine squares with questions or prompts; call on students to answer.	3, 2, 1: Have students write down three things they learned, two things that were interesting or two predictions, and one question they have.	Quick write: Pose a question or state a prompt. Have students write in response, as fast as they can, for two to three minutes.	Acronym or acrostic: Give students a series of letters or allow them to choose their own. Then they start a line or sentence with each letter (related to content).	Haiku or diamante poem: Compose a haiku or diamante based on content.
Whip around: Pose a question or provide a prompt. Quickly move around the room and have each student respond. (Works best with very short answers.)	Red, yellow, green: Have students hold up a sheet of construction paper (or a plastic cup) to indicate their understanding. Red = stop, I don't understand. Yellow = I understand some of it. Green = I get it and am ready to move on!	Word sort: Provide a list of content-area terms. Have students individually sort them based on similarities or other connections. They can share with partners as time allows.	Word splash: Provide a list of content-area terms. Have students write something using as many words as possible.	Inner/outer circle: Form two groups of students, one group as an inner circle facing their peers in the outer circle. Pose a question and allow the partners facing each other to talk. Then rotate and continue.
Gallery walk: Have groups of students create visuals. Hang the visuals. Then have students rotate around to look at all. They can attach Post-it notes or vote on their favorites.	Cloze reading passage: Photocopy or display a short text about recent content with key words/terms left out. Have students provide the words/terms.	Four corners: Provide a question (or several questions) with answers A, B, C, and D. Students walk to the corner that represents their chosen answer.	Agree/disagree: Make a statement. Students line up on either side of the room to indicate whether or not they agree with the statement. Undecided students can stand the middle, and representatives from the two sides can try to persuade them to move.	Tweet: Provide each student with an index card (or a cut-out of the blue Twitter bird). Have them write a tweet on the card. Hold them to the 140-character limit.
Snowball fight: Have students answer a question or respond to a prompt on a sheet of paper. Then they ball up their papers and throw into the air. Each student can pick up a "snowball" to then share in class discussion or write on and throw again.	Venn diagram: Have students list similarities and differences about two concepts, terms, etc.	Entrance or exit ticket: Pose a question or give a prompt. Have students write briefly. Collect these as the start to a lesson or to end the lesson.	Make the test: Have each student create one question that could be used on a test of current content. If time allows, they can partner up and "test" each other.	Make a meme: Provide several photographic images or have students select their own if time allows. Then each student makes a meme from the image (related to content). Students can share as time allows.

Lesson Structure That Includes Formative Assessment

In the previous chapter, you scoped out at least one unit and its learning targets. You outlined the daily lessons and identified at least one co-teaching structure to be used during each lesson. You considered the gradual release of responsibility model and how that impacts lesson design. Now that our topic is formative assessment, let's take a look at how it is an integral part of every lesson that you teach.

The beginning of a lesson is a great time to assess where your students are so that you can adjust your plans in light of what you find out. First, plan your anticipatory set (discussed in the last chapter). Consider the following:

- How will you provide continuity from or connect with previous lessons?

- What key vocabulary could you review or apply?

- Is there an "elevator speech" or "commercial" version of the new material that you can provide—in other words, a thirty-second-to-two-minute overview or "sales pitch" that will get students tuned in?

- How could you activate background knowledge?

- Is there a video that might introduce or elaborate on your content?

These ideas can easily connect to a quick formative assessment. For example, after providing your anticipatory set, you could do any of the following to get a good read on where the students are before you launch into the new material:

- A think-pair-share in which students answer a question or elaborate on the material you presented

- Any type of quick talking or writing activity in which students review and/ or apply some of the key vocabulary

- A quick writing activity in response to a video

- One or two questions that the whole class answers using white boards, hand signals, or an online or electronic method so you instantly know how well they grasp what you covered or how ready they are for new knowledge

After this initial check for understanding, it's time to move into the meat of your lesson. In relation to the gradual release of responsibility model, this is the "I do" section. You and your co-teacher are modeling desired skills and providing new content.

During this segment of the lesson, it's important to integrate more checks for understanding. The longer your lesson, the more you'll need to stop and check so that you know where to go next and who might need a different kind of support.

Which of the following methods do you frequently use during this segment of the lesson? Check all that apply.

- - - - Calling on individual students to answer

- - - - Asking students to hold up white boards or color-coded cards to answer

- - - - Using a digital tool (like Kahoot! or Quizlet) to have students answer questions

- - - - Think-pair-share, elbow partners, or turn-and-talk

- - - - Thumps up/down

- - - - Movement strategies like moving to a corner that designates an answer

- - - - Writing or drawing on a Post-it note or index card, or via some electronic method (for example, using a digital tool like Padlet)

- - - - Taking notes or working sample problems

- - - - Having a student come to the board to demonstrate

- - - - Choral response

- - - - Having students move to stations or centers to talk with others and/or demonstrate what they know and understand

During a workshop I recently facilitated, I was asked how often one should check for understanding in a ninety-minute class. This question got the whole room abuzz, with teachers sharing their ideas and their methods of conducting quick formative assessments. The general consensus, with which I concur, was about every fifteen minutes. This amount of time seems to be reasonable not only for allowing students to stop and process but also for reminding teachers to chunk new information manageably. For shorter class periods, it might be best to stop every ten minutes, and in the primary grades, something even less than ten minutes might be desirable.

After the "I do" portion of any lesson or series of lessons, it's time to move to the "we do" or guided practice portion. This may be a time in which you and your co-teacher will orchestrate group work, workstations, or some other activity that involves students working together or rotating among tasks that involve both cooperative and independent work. The formative assessment that you and your teaching partner do during this part of the lesson should involve a great deal of kid-watching. You'll need to circulate, listen, observe, prompt, cue, and redirect. You'll need to check with each other to plan immediate next steps for both groups and individuals. At some points, one of you may need to provide more direct instruction to a group or to certain individuals, or to provide entirely different content. It is crucial during this guided practice period that every student practice with support what will be done independently later. Therefore, it is imperative that during guided practice, both teachers ensure they check on every student at least once.

Planning for guided practice is something that you and your co-teacher should spend time on daily. You'll need to ensure that students who struggle with reading or who are learning the English language are in groups that support them. You'll need to adapt the content, process, or learning environment not only to help students who need accommodations in these areas but also in order to flexibly group students based on their strengths, weaknesses, and preferences. It may be a good idea to check in with each other after school each day or early in the morning prior to setting up the exact guided practice methods and groups to ensure that you both feel the plan will work smoothly.

For those students who are ready to work independently or at an application level, this is the time when you'll have to differentiate. You and your co-teacher should be ready to move some students to the application-level work sooner than the rest of the class and, if necessary, to provide different work for them as well. The questions about differentiation in the previous chapter should have helped you and your co-teacher envision different options that you can employ.

After guided practice comes independent practice. Sometimes this occurs during the same lesson in which there was guided practice; at other times, it may occur on the following day. It is critical that you informally or formally assess each student during independent practice so that all can be supported toward greater mastery and independence.

In independent practice, it is almost always a good idea to have students create a verbal or written product as evidence of their understanding. This is the time when they need to answer those questions at the end of the chapter or respond to a prompt you and your co-teacher have created. Reference the activity you did earlier ("Thirty Fun, Formative Assessment Ideas") if you feel you've gotten into a rut or would like to try something new.

An important reminder here is that the tasks you ask students to do after independent practice should be directly tied to the learning targets that you developed from your unpacked standards. Any evidence you collect from students about their learning should measure their progress toward the learning targets.

Lastly, for each lesson you'll want to provide some kind of closure "bookended" with the anticipatory set you provided earlier. Keep in mind the learning targets and hit the content that you want to drive home. Use the key vocabulary, show a video clip, ask a provocative question, or orchestrate an activity in which students have to actively apply the knowledge they just gained (something different from what they did in the independent practice segment). If they didn't write anything during the independent practice segment, this would be a good time to use writing in some way—perhaps ask the students to complete an exit ticket or draft a quick summary of what they learned. However, make sure that you emphasize the important content and skills that you want students to know and be able to do. The end of the lesson should serve to bind the learning into the student's brain and body as well as deeply as possible.

Activity: Reflect on the Lesson

When you have time to meet with your partner after teaching a well-constructed lesson, ask yourself the following about each lesson segment:

ANTICIPATORY SET

How did you . . .

- Gain students' attention?

- Make the learning targets or objectives clear?

- Connect to or assess prior learning?

- Build background knowledge if necessary?

- Preteach or identify general academic and domain-specific vocabulary that was critical in the lesson?

MODELING

How did you . . .

- Explain new concepts?

- Use visuals, objects, multimedia, etc. in your explanations?

- Highlight key vocabulary?

GUIDED PRACTICE

How did you . . .

- Provide practice opportunities?

- Allow for social interaction?

- Use scaffolding?

- Differentiate?

- Support students in self-regulation and self-assessment?

INDEPENDENT PRACTICE

How did you . . .

- Determine who was ready to move on and who needed further support?

- Extend learning for those who were advanced?

- Differentiate?

- Support students in self-regulation and self-assessment?

How did you . . .

- Emphasize or review the most important content and skills?

- Make connections to future lessons?

- Emphasize real-world, practical applications or connections?

- Promote further inquiry?

Assessment Considerations for Co-Taught Classes

If at all possible, both co-teachers should be involved in creating formative and summative assessments. In the last chapter, you and your co-teacher may have experimented with the overall design of a summative assessment, or you may have even created the assessment itself. Co-creating summative assessments can be a very valuable activity. If you're a general education teacher who has not been part of a team developing assessments together, getting feedback and critique from another professional can help you see your content in a new light. Also, you may find that the way you structure items, state directions, or even lay out a page could be tweaked for greater effectiveness.

Obviously, in some grade levels and courses, summative assessments are dictated by district curriculum guides. If this is the case, use these summative assessments as a guide. You and your co-teaching partner can collaboratively plan backwards from these high-stakes measures and create a series of formative assessments that are well integrated with your daily lessons. These formative assessments allow students to practice and allow you to change instruction to help them reach their highest levels of achievement on the final measure.

Some students need to receive their legally required accommodations on assessments that impact their grades (in most cases, summative assessments). Both of you should bounce ideas off each other to best plan for how all your co-taught students can be successful on any assignments that count significantly toward their grades. On formative assessments, students may not want or need the accommodations they are entitled to. Be sure to find out what their preferences are. It's always best to let students attempt on-grade-level work without accommodations or adult support if they wish to; their increasing confidence can positively impact their competence!

The Value of Pre-Assessment

When beginning a new unit of instruction, it may be helpful to give a pre-assessment to determine where all your students are in relation to the learning targets. If you have a predetermined curriculum that provides pre-assessments, then by all means, use them! If, however, you don't have these available to you, you and your co-teaching partner can certainly create them if you feel they would be of benefit.

A pre-assessment can be used to assess students' mastery of prerequisites, general understanding of critical terminology, and familiarity with new, on-grade-level material. Often teachers don't want to create a pre-assessment based solely on the new, on-grade-level material because they fear their students will find the assessment too difficult. My advice to these teachers is to start the assessment with a few items about content, vocabulary, and skills that should have been mastered previously and put the "not yet taught" items toward the end. In this way, you can see by how far each student attempts to answer down the page exactly where the student hits her or his limit.

Another option is to teach some new content, perhaps for a few days, and then give a short, formal, formative assessment before proceeding with additional new content. Using a series of short formatives like this throughout a unit can help students prepare bit by bit for the summative assessment.

Tool 1 at the end of this chapter provides a process to create a pre-assessment for any unit.

Conclusion

Formative assessment runs the gamut from the moment-by-moment observation teachers do of children to the planned, formal tasks that are administered to measure progress toward articulated learning targets.

The following process can be used to create a pre-assessment for the beginning of any unit, before significant teaching has occurred. The results of the pre-assessment can be used to differentiate instruction and form groups.

1. Unpack the standard(s).

2. Create learning targets.

3. Sequence the learning targets from the least complex/difficult to the most complex/difficult.

4. Examine the first few learning targets. Ask yourself:

   - What is the prerequisite knowledge and skills students must have before accessing this new content?

   - What general academic and domain-specific vocabulary should students have mastered before accessing this new content?

5. Draft items that assess the prerequisite knowledge, skills, and vocabulary.

Here is the thinking of one co-teaching pair:

Standard: Determine the main idea of a text and explain how it is supported by key details; summarize the text. (CCSS RI 4.2)

Unpacked standard:

Determine the main idea of an informational text.

Explain how the main idea is supported by key details. (This implies determining which details are key versus which are of lesser importance.)

Summarize an informational text.

Possible learning targets, sequenced in order of complexity:

I know that the main idea of an informational text is the point the author is trying to make or what the author is trying to teach us about the subject.

I know that the main idea of a text is often stated clearly in a sentence or two.

I can identify key details from the text.

I can use key details from the text to determine the main idea.

I know that a summary contains only the most important details.

I can explain how the key details support the main idea.

I can use details and the main idea to write an accurate summary.

Prerequisite knowledge and skills required:

Students must understand how informational texts differ from other texts, especially narrative.

Students need to be able to differentiate between main ideas and key details. They need to know that a main idea is overarching and that details are subordinate to main ideas.

Students need to know that some ideas directly support the main idea and some are only loosely related.

Students need to understand that in a summary only the most important details are included.

Vocabulary that should have been mastered:

Informational text

Main idea

Detail

Summary

Items that assess prerequisite knowledge, skills, and vocabulary:

1. Which of the following types of text tells a story?

    a. opinion

    b. narrative (correct answer)

    c. informational

2. Which of the following types of text explains something?

    a. opinion

    b. narrative

    c. informational (correct answer)

3. What is the main idea of an informational text?

    a. the lesson the reader is supposed to learn

    b. what the text is mostly about (correct answer)

    c. the author's opinion about something

(Continued)

(Continued)

4. What kinds of details appear in informational texts? Mark all that apply.

   a. facts (correct)

   b. setting

   c. characters

   d. examples (correct)

   e. statistics (correct)

   f. anecdotes (correct)

   g. similes

5. What is a summary?

   a. someone's opinion about a story

   b. notes about a topic studied

   c. a short version of an informational text (correct answer)

online resources ⟋ This resource can be found at http://resources.corwin.com/coteachersplaybook

Appendix A

A BRIEF HISTORY OF CO-TEACHING

Co-teaching situations are increasingly common as educators try to meet the wide range of learning needs of students. According to statistics from the National Center for Education (2018a, 2018b), approximately 9.5% of students in the United States are English language learners and 12.9% have specific learning disabilities. Theoretically, one could walk into any classroom in America and find that 20% of the total number of students possess a wide variety of special needs. Your classroom may be one of these. If you teach in an urban location, your numbers may be even higher.

The movement to include special education students (and, later, students facing other conditions and circumstances) began in the late 1960s so that as many students as possible would have full access to a regular education program and would not experience segregation from their peers. This movement, initially driven by parents, resulted in the Individuals with Disabilities Education Act (IDEA). This act is the updated version of Public Law 94-142, which included two fundamentals: a free, appropriate education (FAPE) in the least restrictive environment (LRE).

IDEA was first signed into law in 1975. It has been revised and expanded several times since. The most recent amendments came in 2004, with the final regulations for preschool and school-age children published in 2006 and those for infants and toddlers in 2011. The U.S. Department of Education maintains a robust site about IDEA at http://idea.ed.gov.

Past efforts to meet the special needs of students went under the labels *mainstreaming* and *inclusion*. Mainstreaming was the effort to mix special needs students who were being served in separate classrooms back into general education classes. It was assumed that these students would be able to find success once mainstreamed; however, without also having specialized assistance within the regular education classes, many students struggled.

Inclusion was the next wave of reform, and, in its most ideal approaches, it approximated effective co-teaching. Special needs students were placed in general education classes but were also supported by specialists. As inclusion evolved, the term *co-teaching* became more pervasive and accurate as it more clearly denotes the relationship that the general ed teacher and the specialist must have so that all students perform well. In much of the research literature of recent years, the term *inclusive settings* is used to describe a school's or system's efforts to include all children in the regular education setting as much as possible during the school day. *Co-teaching* is used to describe the arrangement by which some of a school's teachers instruct so that all learners can be successful.

The "pushing-in" of specialists to support students who have special needs continues to gain popularity not only because federal legislation has moved in that direction but also because it is now generally accepted that most students, regardless of learning disability or language fluency, deserve maximum access to the general curriculum and to interaction with their age-like peers.

Appendix B

One teach, one assist

One teach, one observe

Alternative teaching

Parallel teaching

Station teaching

Team teaching

Appendix C

Ways to paraphrase:

- If I'm understanding you correctly, you said/feel/want . . .

- So you were angry/upset/frustrated/concerned when . . .

- You're thinking . . .

- You're wondering . . .

- To put it another way, one might say . . .

- What is important to you is . . .

Effective ways to summarize include:

- Your main points/concerns are . . .

- So there's a difference between _ _ _ _ _ and _ _ _ _ _.

- The theme/pattern that has emerged here is . . .

- To state your position in one sentence, one might say . . .

- Overall, you're saying that . . .

- Basically, your point is . . .

Effective ways to affirm and/or check for accuracy include:

- (Summarize what the other person said.) Is that correct?

- _ _ _ _ _ is a valid point.

- That's an interesting idea. Let's explore it a bit more.

- I understand where you're coming from.

- I hadn't thought of _ _ _ _ _ before. Thank you for that idea.

Appendix D

The most awesome co-teaching team
ever is busy having our
VERY IMPORTANT regular meeting!
Please...

DO
NOT
DISTURB

We look forward to speaking
with you at another time!

 This resource can be found at http://resources.corwin.com/coteachersplaybook

We are
UNAVAILABLE
at this time!

We are engaged in

VERY IMPORTANT work that

will benefit our students.

Please come back

after _ _ _ _ _ _ _ _ _ _ _ _

References

Ainsworth, L. (2006). Unwrapping the standards [Presentation]. Retrieved from https://www.mbaea.org/media/documents/Unwrapping_STDs_Ainsworth_FAE6BD257ADAE.pdf

Anderson, L. W., Krathwohl, D. R., & Bloom, B. S. (2001). *A taxonomy for learning, teaching, and assessing: A revision of Bloom's Taxonomy of educational objectives* (Complete ed.). New York, NY: Longman.

Beninghof, A. M. (2012). *Co-teaching that works: Structures and strategies for maximizing student learning.* San Francisco, CA: Jossey-Bass.

Black, P., & Wiliam, D. (1998). Assessment and classroom learning. *Assessment in Education: Principles, Policy, and Practice, 5*(1), 7–73.

Bogel, A. (2017). *Reading people: How seeing the world through the lens of personality changes everything.* Grand Rapids, MI: Baker Books.

Cook, L., & Friend, M. (1995). Co-teaching: Guidelines for creating effective practices. *Focus on Exceptional Children, 28*(3), 1–17.

Curry School of Education. (2012). Co-teaching defined. Retrieved from http://faculty.virginia.edu/coteaching/definition.html

DuFour, R., & Reeves, D. (2016). The futility of PLC lite. *Phi Delta Kappan, 97*(6), 70.

Frayer, D. A., Frederick, W. C., & Klausmeier, H. J. (1969). *A schema for testing the level of concept mastery: Report from the Project on Situational Variables and Efficiency of Concept Learning.* Madison: Wisconsin Research and Development Center for Cognitive Learning.

Friend, M. (2007). Co-teaching defined. Retrieved from http://www.marilynfriend.com/basics.htm

Garcia, J. (2018a). Co-teaching jitters. Retrieved from https://justingarciaell.com/coteachingjitters/

Garcia, J. (2018b). 2018 co-teaching reflection. Retrieved from https://justingarciaell.com/2018-co-teaching-reflection/

Gonzalez, J. (2014). Know your terms: Anticipatory set. [Web log post]. Retrieved from https://www.cultofpedagogy.com/anticipatory-set/

Gonzalez, J. (2016). Classroom management: 4 keys to starting the year off right [Web log post]. Retrieved from https://www.cultofpedagogy.com/classroom-management-plan/

Gonzalez, J. (2018). Twelve ways to upgrade your classroom design. [Web log post]. Retrieved from https://www.cultofpedagogy.com/upgrade-classroom-design

McTighe, J., & Wiggins, G. (2013). *Essential questions: Opening doors to student understanding.* Alexandria, VA: Association for Supervision and Curriculum Development. Retrieved from http://www.ascd.org/publications/books/109004/chapters/What-Makes-a-Question-Essential%A2.aspx

Murawski, W., & Swanson, H. (2001). A meta-analysis of co-teaching research: Where are the data? *Remedial and Special Education, 22*(5), 258–267.

National Center for Education Statistics. (2018a). Fast facts: English language learners. Retrieved from https://nces.ed.gov/fastfacts/display.asp?id=96

National Center for Education Statistics. (2018b). Fast facts: Students with disabilities. Retrieved from https://nces.ed.gov/fastfacts/display.asp?id=64

Pearson, P. D., & Gallagher, G. (1983). The gradual release of responsibility model of instruction. *Contemporary Educational Psychology, 8*, 112–123.

Popham, J. (2008). *Transformative assessment*. Alexandria, VA: ASCD.

Power-DeFur, L. A., & Orelove, F. P. (1997). *Inclusive education: Practical implementation of the least restrictive environment*. Gaithersburg, MD: Aspen Publishers.

Rosenthal, H., & Zindler, R., Teaching2gether, LLC. (2015). Intro to Marilyn Friend's co-teaching models: The big picture. Retrieved from http://www.teaching2gethertexas.com/uploads/4/5/2/9/45296987/introtoco-teachingapproachesthebigpicture.pdf

Sacks, A. (2014). Eight tips for making the most of co-teaching [Web log entry]. Retrieved from https://www.edweek.org/tm/articles/2014/10/15/ctq_sacks_coteaching.html?r=6768781

Sharpe, W. (n.d.). Special education inclusion. *Education World*. Retrieved from https://www.educationworld.com/a_curr/curr320.shtml

Trites, N. (2017). What is co-teaching? An introduction to co-teaching and inclusion. Retrieved from http://castpublishing.org/introduction-co-teaching-inclusion/

Vagle, N. D. (2015). *Design in five: Essential phases to create engaging assessment practice*. Bloomington, IN: Solution Tree.

Van Garderen, D., Stormont, M., & Goel, N. (2012). Collaboration between general and special educators and student outcomes: A need for more research. *Psychology in the Schools, 49*(5). Retrieved from http://onlinelibrary.wiley.com/wol1/doi/10.1002/pits.21610/full

Webb, N. (November 2005). Depth-of-knowledge levels for four content areas. Presentation to the Florida Education Research Association, 50th Annual Meeting, Miami, Florida.

Wiggins, G. (2010). What is a big idea? [Web log entry]. Retrieved from http://www.authenticeducation.org/ae_bigideas/article.lasso?artid=99

Wiggins, G., & McTighe, J. (2012). *The understanding by design guide to advanced concepts in creating and reviewing units*. Alexandria, VA: ASCD. Retrieved from https://pdo.ascd.org/lmscourses/PD12OC002/media/CCSS_UBD_M2_Reading_Unpacking_Standards.pdf

Wisconsin Department of Public Instruction. (n.d.). Co-teaching in Wisconsin. Retrieved from https://dpi.wi.gov/sped/educators/consultation/co-teaching

Wong, H. K., & Wong, R. T. (1998). *The first days of school*. Mountain View, CA: Wong Publications, Inc.

Index

No matter where you are in your professional journey, Corwin aims to ease the many demands teachers face on a daily basis with accessible strategies that benefit ALL learners. Through research-based, high-quality content, we offer practical guidance on a wide range of topics, including curriculum planning, learning frameworks, classroom design and management, and much more. Our books, videos, consulting, and online resources are developed by renowned educators and designed for easy implementation that will provide tangible results for you and your students.

CAITLIN KRAUSE

Mindful by Design provides 24 detailed exercises for teachers and students, including step-by-step mindfulness lessons embedded into specific curriculum areas, ready to implement immediately.

JOHN ANTONETTI AND TERRI STICE

Use the Powerful Task Rubric for Designing Student Work to analyze, design, and refine engaging tasks of learning.

CAROL PELLETIER RADFORD

This newly revised workbook-style resource provides a robust companion website featuring videos, downloadable forms, and a digital Mentor Planning Guide and Journal for reflection.

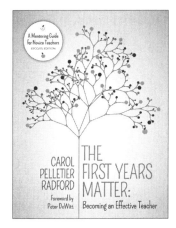

CAROL PELLETIER RADFORD

This second edition prepares new teachers for the rigors and expectations of the classroom and includes mentor-teacher strategies, a flexible twelve-month curriculum, companion website, and more!

CORWIN

TMN195F8

A SAGE Publishing Company

Helping educators make the greatest impact

CORWIN HAS ONE MISSION: to enhance education through intentional professional learning.

We build long-term relationships with our authors, educators, clients, and associations who partner with us to develop and continuously improve the best evidence-based practices that establish and support lifelong learning.